COMMUNE:
LIFE IN RURAL CHINA

COMMUNE:
LIFE IN
RURAL CHINA

PEGGY PRINTZ and PAUL STEINLE
Illustrated with photographs by the authors

DODD, MEAD & COMPANY · NEW YORK

1 2 3 4 5 6 7 8 9 10

Library of Congress Cataloging in Publication Data

Printz, Peggy.
    Commune : life in rural China.

    Bibliography: p.
    1. Communes (China)—Case studies. I. Steinle,
Paul, joint author. II. Title.
JS7352.P75   334′.683′0951   76–58427
ISBN 0–396–07420–0

TO GENE PELL
and our friends from the
Group W foreign news service

ACKNOWLEDGMENTS

We gratefully acknowledge the cooperation of the following friends and associates: Steven Goldstein, Professor of Government, Smith College, Northampton, Massachusetts; Sydney Liu, *Newsweek,* Hong Kong; R. V. Pandit, Publisher, The Perennial Press, Hong Kong; William L. Parish, Professor of Sociology, University of Chicago, Chicago, Illinois; Shelby Schuck, Boston, Massachusetts; Vivienne Shue, Assistant Professor, Political Science Department, Yale University, New Haven, Connecticut; Martin Whyte, Professor of Sociology, University of Michigan, Ann Arbor, Michigan; and the Staff of the American Consulate General in Hong Kong.

Special appreciation goes to the Westinghouse Broadcasting Company, which sponsored our trip to China.

CONTENTS

INTRODUCTION

During the spring growing season of 1973, as Chinese Communist Party Chairman Mao Tse-tung gazed beatifically from his portrait on the wall of the administrative committee meeting room at Kwang Li People's Commune, he beheld an unusual scene. Instead of the usual gathering of officials, Mao's faded photograph surveyed a collection of photographic lighting cases, audio tapes, batteries, metal suitcases, and cardboard boxes, which spilled across table tops, along benches, and onto the stone floor. Our television documentary film crew had converted the meeting room into storage space for film and camera equipment. Here in the inner sanctum of commune headquarters, we would collect our equipment each morning; and here we would return at noon, sagging with fatigue, to reassemble our supplies for the afternoon's shooting. And before we went to sleep on the hot May nights, we would deposit the heavy equipment under the watchful eyes of Chairman Mao's photograph.

Coming as it did during the height of Sino-American détente, our visit provided an unprecedented opportunity to observe life in rural China, relatively unrestricted. Aiding our flexibility was the size of our group—only three persons: two Americans—the producer, Paul Steinle, Westinghouse Broadcasting Company's bureau chief in Hong Kong; the associate producer, his wife, freelance journalist Peggy Printz—and Hong Kong cinematographer Tony Munday, an Australian citizen.

The three of us had spent an accumulated total of sixteen years living, traveling, and working in Southeast Asia, so we brought to our China encounters some perspective on the region and its problems. Thus we could compare a Chinese peasant farmer to his counterpart in Java or Luzon, tilling the soil by hand, rather than to an Ohio corn farmer with a fleet of International Harvesters in his barn. And we could inspect

Kwang Li's hospital with an awareness of the state of health care in the villages of Vietnam and Bengal.

After visiting Kwang Li briefly in November 1972, while reporting for Group W (Westinghouse) radio news from the Canton Trade Fair, Paul Steinle had envisioned a television documentary "introducing American audiences to a people's commune." His written request for us to film at Kwang Li was specifically couched in those terms.

After the Foreign Ministry in Peking granted our visa request, we began a month of research and discussions with China scholars in Hong Kong. We filled a ring-binder notebook with nearly seven hundred questions.

At Kwang Li, Commune Vice-Chairman Liang Wei-ming and—during the first few days—Chairman Liang Nien led the reception committee that accompanied us everywhere. There were also two inter-preters from the China International Travel Service, Mr. Huang (pro-nounced *Wong*) and Mr. Wen; and two drivers—a crewcut minibus conductor, who insisted on speeding down the country roads honking at everything in sight, and a lanky, taciturn chauffeur for the interpret-ers' car. The regular entourage also included an official of the adminis-trative area, who was responsible for foreign visitors. He was a dignified gentleman who smiled graciously with unruffled aplomb and offered his sympathy whenever the cameras would jam, the tape recorder would fail, or the lights would flicker out. Huang Lien-tsi, of the commune women's department, provided responses to our questions about wo-men's roles, as well as constantly brandishing a thermos of lukewarm tea, clean cups, and a raft of towels. And sometimes we were joined by Ma Ping-kuan, the chief administrator of the Sui Kang production brigade, who often came along for the ride. So our excursions within Kwang Li resembled a V.I.P. motorcade as we roared through the rice fields. It was nearly impossible to avoid attracting attention even when we abandoned the cars, which were the only passenger vehicles on the commune, since we were constantly accompanied by our coterie of escorts.

In spite of the entourage, which eventually diminished as the days wore on, we were free to travel wherever we wished at Kwang Li and to ask whatever questions we could think of posing to the commune's forty-three thousand residents.

After about a week, our entourage from commune headquarters began to tire. One day, after a particularly exhausting cinematic chase through farms and factories, we set out to film scenes of daily life in a village. To our surprise, our hosts decided to wait in the car on the outskirts of the village. So we wandered alone along the village paths shooting film, as a few peasants eyed us in curious but polite silence. We returned to the car to find most of the official escort party dozing inside. They were just too tired to bother with us any longer! We were exhausted, too, but determined to make the best use of every moment.

Our hosts never requested to see our film before or after we edited it in Hong Kong during the summer months that followed. In fact, the China International Travel Service helped us ship half of our film, undeveloped, out of China before our departure. We carried with us the remaining rolls of exposed, undeveloped film when we left China. Never did any Chinese officials suggest that we show them the film, nor did any of them even mention the possibility of screening the finished film. Many months later, after the film, entitled *Commune,* was telecast over the Westinghouse Broadcasting Company stations in the U.S.A. (as well as on educational stations and several European networks), we invited the New China News Agency representatives in Hong Kong to a screening and shipped a copy of the film and our published articles to the Foreign Ministry in Peking. Perhaps, the CCP officials reasoned, there was not much we could film that would be offensive—especially under the supervision of our diligent hosts. However no one could disguise all the "warts" in such a large area.

No commune residents refused to answer our questions—though it was sometimes necessary to persist to get at the truth.

"Who presents the greatest threat to women's emancipation, men or women?" we queried of feminist Huang Lien-tsi.

"In the remote areas, there are still some forces that don't like exact equality. . . ." she replied.

"What do you mean by 'forces'?"

"Incorrect thinking," she said, explaining that, for instance, men might look down on illiterate women.

"Does incorrect thinking exist equally among both men and women?"

"Yes."

"Among which group, men or women, is the problem more serious?"

"Well, we could say that this incorrect thinking is more serious among women," came the roundabout answer.

We spent virtually all our waking hours at Kwang Li, filming or interviewing, some days from 8:00 A.M. until past 10:00 at night. Though they often laughed, especially when we inquired into their personal lives, the people did not appear to resent the time we spent interrogating them or the tenor of our questions. Perhaps our own halting attempts at direct contact in elementary Chinese helped to establish warmth and rapport before the interpreters launched into the serious questions.

The commune was accessible, and we filmed at will. As a result, we left confident that we had been given a rare opportunity to create a complete, fair journalistic record of life in rural China.

COMMUNE:
LIFE IN RURAL CHINA

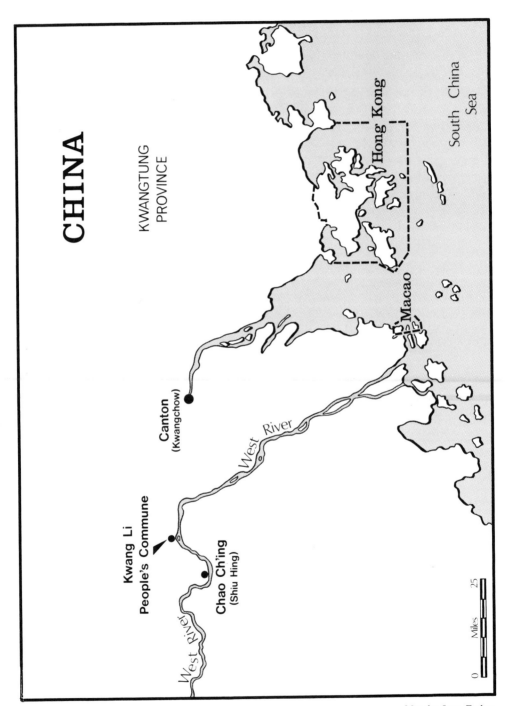

Map by Joan Forbes

1
IMPRESSIONS

In the dappled noontime shade of a village tree, two young women in flowered aprons took turns combing each other's hair and fastening it with ribbons. Their sing-song chatter mingled with the whack of a heavy steel knife slapping against a wooden block, as someone prepared vegetables for lunch. Suddenly, a rush of static crackled through the sleepy village, followed by the pulse of military music. The commune's broadcasting station was beginning its noon program. From loudspeakers wired to each house and public building, a brittle voice recited the government version of the news.

Rural China presented a curious mixture of such contradictory images—the natural and the regimented, the informal and the official, the old and the new.

The individuality, flexibility, and vibrant humanity of the Chinese countryside contrasted sharply with the stereotyped images of drab, gray automatons which had symbolized Chinese Communist Party Chairman Mao Tse-tung's brave new world to the American psyche. We were surprised, relieved, to find unstarched attitudes and even gaiety, in a setting which our mind's eye had conceived as monochromatic and regimented. Discovering China was like bracing for a fall but unexpectedly plopping into a feather cushion.

Rarely have Western journalists stayed longer than an afternoon at a people's commune. We enjoyed the privilege of spending enough time to see what we considered flaws as well as virtues.

What we found contrasted starkly with our preconceived images of militant masses of Chinese scurrying mechanically through their chores. Instead, the pace in China's countryside was surprisingly slow. The most hectic activity at Kwang Li People's Commune came from the passenger buses that rumbled down the dirt road which stretched between parallel lines of slender trees, connecting the main highway to

Here Peggy Printz interviews a field worker through interpreter Huang.

the commune center. Just as elsewhere in Asia, buses careened down the road with disdain for peasants on bicycles or on foot. Pigs, chickens, and geese scattered frantically from their path like spray arching before the prow of a boat.

Where was the authoritarian China we had anticipated? Where were the bleak legions marching in forced step and, worse still, where was the enforced thought control? We were not to find that Cold War China. The new China was harmonious and *not* always homogeneous, and the people were free enough to conduct productive, yet leisurely lives. When we did encounter rigid Communist rule, it was in subtle forms: a firm, almost blind adherence to principle, a dialogue that did not allow room for doubt, an overwhelming acceptance where questions only led to a limited range of answers.

Yet these restrictions meant little to the people of Kwang Li. Perhaps in China's cities, where freer intellectual ferment once flourished, the new order narrowed horizons. But in the countryside, the channeled ideology of Communism embodied a better way of life than the peasants had previously known. Most Kwang Li residents had not before been able to read or write, let alone consider abstract political ideals. For many of Kwang Li's peasants, their first chance to participate in their society in any large sense came on the heels of the Communist victory, when for the first time they were given a voice to express their condition.

For them, Communism was identified with an emancipation of sorts. And along with the new ruling order came an even more revolutionary concept: security. The peasants had enough to eat, they enjoyed protection from natural disaster and disease, and they were learning to utilize rather than to fear the elements. All this appeared to mean much more to the peasants of the new China than any political concepts or ideological strictures.

In our own Cold War childhoods, we'd heard grisly tales of forced family separation. We looked for evidence that Communism had destroyed the most important element of Chinese culture: the family. We found instead that the new era had brought strengthened nuclear family ties for most Chinese by giving women a new prestige. However, broader kinship ties, particularly clan allegiances, were weakened.

As for the reputed poverty of Mao's China, if it existed, it was not a salient feature of life at Kwang Li. Certainly there were ramshackle houses, ragged clothing, and cramped living quarters on this commune.

But we found little of the squalor and despair, and none of the endemic disease, malnutrition, and degradation we'd seen elsewhere in heavily populated areas of Southeast Asia, conditions which also typified the China of the past. Everyone had enough to eat, access to medical care, and a rudimentary but stable dwelling. It was a far cry from the shanty villages and indigent labor which characterized much of developing Asia. What had transpired was a giant leap from the China of just a generation ago.

At Kwang Li we were to observe many events and hear many conversations that generally substantiated our belief in this progress. Repeatedly we were impressed that these peasants, who were eyewitnesses to one of the most momentous social upheavals in history, had personally experienced the effects of that revolution in every aspect of their lives. Keeping in mind what Kwang Li was like before the Communists took over in 1949, we were to evaluate the sacrifices that made China's success possible.

In China's southern province of Kwangtung, the farming and market community known as Kwang Li nestles between humpbacked hills and the bank of the broad West River. The river rises in the mountains far to the northwest, races past Kwang Li to the huge industrial city of Canton (Kwangchow) fifty-five miles to the east, and eventually spills into the South China Sea. This agricultural area served as the exemplary microcosm for our introduction to rural China.

Because of its ideal river location, Kwang Li town naturally developed over centuries as a bustling market center for peasant farmers from the villages in the surrounding rice fields, and as a thriving port for river commerce.

Kwang Li functioned as an administrative entity many decades before the Communists arrived. Under China's previous governments, Kwang Li town and the smaller settlements in its immediate environment were called a *hsiang*. Such a cluster of villages, an "administrative village," was akin to a township in the rural United States.[1]

China's Communist leaders changed much about Kwang Li and the rural way of life. But they preserved many features of this ancient community, including its name. Nowadays, though, Kwang Li has a new title. It is designated a people's commune. All of rural China, where 80 to 85 percent of the country's population dwells, is divided into approximately seventy-five thousand people's communes.

The quality of life in these people's communes varies dramatically from region to region across the vastness of the People's Republic of China. So does the size of the people's communes. Kwang Li's population of forty-three thousand was an average for southern China. Many people's communes supported populations half again as large. But the basic institutions at Kwang Li—its administrative and political milieu, its systems of education and health care—are reflected throughout the country. These institutions are the products of the Chinese Communist Party (CCP), and the influence of the CCP dominates everywhere in China. That is why examining the people's commune at Kwang Li provides a basic understanding of the lifestyle practiced by the majority of the Chinese people.

Kwang Li provides a particularly good example, because it is one of China's "model soldier" people's communes. On these settlements, the Chinese leaders conduct pilot programs, in agriculture or education, for example. Thus Kwang Li's residents enjoy advantages over some of their neighbors. However, although Kwang Li is a showcase, it is not atypical. There are thousands of model communes across China. Besides, en route to Kwang Li we passed other people's communes where the lifestyle appeared roughly comparable to that at Kwang Li.

Although CCP directives emanate from Peking, by the time the instructions are put into practice in the countryside, many individuals have interpreted and modified the official commands. The directives are also altered by such factors as local conditions and peasant attitudes. As a result, a CCP dictum such as "Seek self-sufficiency" may be observed in a thousand different ways. Some people may even ignore it! So we were surprised to find that China was not an ideological Great Wall. National creeds lent themselves to infinite modification. Individuals and communities could mold the system, within certain boundaries, to suit personal and local needs.

Drastic changes have transpired at Kwang Li since 1958, when the people's commune was formed, particularly in the local form of government. The commune administration has nurtured (force-fed, some might argue) the political awareness of the people and developed their consciousness along certain lines, so that the relationship between the peasants and the government is much more intimate and complex than anyone might have dreamed just a few decades ago.

Yet many aspects of rural society remain unchanged at Kwang Li. The peasants fulfill many of the same daily tasks and follow many of the ancient patterns of Chinese life that originated in their country's most distant history. CCP officials have been obliged to preserve those features of rural life which they felt served a purpose, or which the peasants were unwilling to abandon. Just as at Kwang Li the party took advantage of the peasants' traditional *economic* market community, so too, the new rulers of China often molded their *political* innovations to fit within the indigenous rural culture.

When Communism surged through China, in the cities and some rural areas, there was resistance, flight, renunciation. But for the most part the peasants had little to lose, and the new way of life demonstrated promise, so the vast majority conformed to create a new order.

2
FAMILIES

It was nearly noon and Huang (Wong) Si-kuan was preparing lunch in the stone kitchen shed across the courtyard from her family's living quarters.[2] She drew a heavy steel chopping knife from its bamboo sheath on the kitchen wall and set to work slicing a pile of shiny green melons on a wooden block. Almost without looking, with the ease of long habit, she chopped off the ends, split the cucumberlike vegetables lengthwise, and scooped out the seeds. With a steady rhythm of clean, tiny strokes, she sliced the melons into thin, crescent-shaped pieces.

Her kitchen was a tiny room charred by generations of cooking fires. Attired in a drab, loose-fitting black shirt and rolled-up trousers, the common uniform of Chinese peasant women her age (fifty), Huang worked amid drifting smoke. With her hair sleekly drawn into a bun at the base of her slim neck, she presented a chiaroscuro figure against a shaft of light from a hole in the ceiling, a vent where the smoke curled lazily skywards.

Like many women in Sui Kang village on Kwang Li People's Commune, Huang Si-kuan was not a native of this village. She was born in a neighboring market area. When she was about sixteen (she could not remember exactly), she came to this region as a handicrafts artisan. Here she met Chen Chi-fun, a peasant four years her senior, whom she married three years later. (In China, women kept their maiden names.) Since it was the custom for Chinese women to settle with their in-laws, she moved into the Chen house, where she lived to this day.

The Chens' family life provided an example of one of the major surprises for foreigners visiting China in the 1970s. For despite the changes commune living had dictated, Chinese country life still centered around the nuclear family. Although they no longer farmed their personal land for a living, families like the Chens still lived and ate together.

Nevertheless, Sui Kang village had changed radically since Huang Si-kuan moved here as a bride in the early 1940s. The transformation of family life was an integral goal of the Chinese Communist Party (CCP) program, so as soon as they had laid their administrative foundations in the rural areas after 1949, Communist officials set about proselytizing for their new way of life.

In the countryside, significant alterations in family relationships followed the replacement of family-clan farming with collective field labor. Previously, common cultivation had reinforced the bonds of kinship.

At about the same time, in 1950, a nationwide marriage law was instituted. This law, combined with the collectivization of family land, ended arranged marriages—a feudal practice often motivated by the desire for land tenure and the consolidation of two families' landholdings.

The 1950 law also abolished such cruel practices as forced marriages, marriages to children, and marriages to deceased persons (a method of perpetuating the rites of ancestor worship). Supposedly, the payment of a bride price was also prohibited. The law and the new collective farming system eroded the traditional tyranny of the older generation. No longer were the husband's parents permitted to escape blame when they mistreated a young wife, claiming they had purchased rights to her. In the old society, such abuses had in some cases driven young women to suicide.

By the time the people's communes were officially established in 1958, the strong bonds to the land that held family clans together had been eradicated; but nuclear families still pooled their incomes and shared their expenditures. Theoretically, each family member came to participate more in decision making. In contrast, in the past the elder patriarchs played the dominant role in familial authority.

But tradition dies hard. As one daughter-in-law in her early twenties told us, "When it comes to big things, of course the parents decide."

Neighborhood work teams eventually took the place of the clans in rural Chinese society. The altar and ancestor portraits that had sanctified family continuity were replaced. In the Chen household, a poster depicting a beneficent Chairman Mao commanded the place of honor that formerly was reserved for the family patriarch.

In all of China, CCP-initiated changes caused the greatest upheaval in the rural areas. In the cities, the cohesive strength of the Chinese family had been disintegrating since the early 1900s, whereas the conversion of the rural population often took years, so ingrained were the old traditions. But for the most part, the new order appeared to be well-established in Kwang Li People's Commune.

Ultimately, the nuclear family unit survived these transformations and remained the basic social and residential institution of commune life. In the late 1950s, life at Kwang Li, as in many other people's communes, had been typified by the gang labor of mobile water-works brigades; and during 1958, the commune had attempted a brief experiment with communal dining halls. But the work brigades had been eliminated when major water conservation projects had been completed in 1959; and communal dining had failed, simply because in those days, the commune could not produce enough food to give all the people as much as they desired.

Ever since then, families had taken their meals at their own hearthsides. Gone were the stark dormitories and mess halls that lingered in the whispered memory of the early days of CCP rule. At Kwang Li, all that remained of that period were small volunteer work groups such as one that we encountered living in a construction dormitory in the hills.

Despite the measures enacted through the marriage law, especially those involving the emancipation of women, which seemed radical to Chinese peasants, the new Chinese leaders were careful to avoid disturbing those family customs which the CCP perceived as healthy and which left many minor responsibilities, such as child care, with the family rather than the State.

Many family-oriented traditions were allowed to persist, provided they did not disrupt commune life and production. The CCP stripped the Chinese New Year celebration of its religious trappings and rituals; but they preserved this family feast and gave it a new name, Spring Festival.

As before, tradition and convenience dictated that young women live with their husbands' families. So Huang Si-kuan's eldest daughter, who married a man from another people's commune, went there to live.

"I rarely see her or her three children," said Huang softly, her lips curved in a smile but her eyes wistful.

When lunch was ready and steaming, Huang Si-kuan carried a pot of soup to the dining area and returned for dishes of meat and vegetables. One by one, the members of the Chen family filed into the kitchen to scoop rice from one of several drumlike bamboo steamers into their deep bowls. Then they carried them across the open courtyard to the dining table. The father, Chen Chi-fun, a surveyor, took the seat of honor across from the salted fish and helped himself to a pungent morsel. This dish has always been popular among Chinese peasants because a little goes a long way to season the bland, cooked rice.

Chen's eldest son, Yung-chai, joined his father and started piling vegetables on his rice. This twenty-four-year-old worked for a village bamboo factory. His wife, Tan Wu, twenty-two, and the second Chen son, twenty-one-year-old Yung-tien, both agricultural workers, arrived with their rice bowls brimming. They were joined by the two youngest Chens, thirteen-year-old Yung-tsin and his ten-year-old sister, Su-ching.

"I wish you one day . . . nine bowls of rice," sings a character in the Chinese revolutionary opera *Sha Chia Pang,* about a future Chinese utopia. As the Chen family dined, it was evident why a full rice bowl symbolized prosperity and stability in China. They devoured their rice, treating their meat and vegetables merely as condiments for this staple. Even at breakfast time, the family ate rice, either steamed or as a watery gruel known as *congee.* In this community, as in all of China, the phrase *"sic fan,"* which literally translates "eat rice," was the idiom to say "Let's eat."

Though the Chen family talked little as they ate, the room was not silent. Wooden chopsticks and ceramic spoons clinked against rice bowls and central serving dishes. Occasionally there was a squawk or flutter from a chicken pecking under the table; and the strains of a martial anthem emanating from a loudspeaker on the wall heralded the noontime news broadcast from the commune's public-address system. Although they could switch off the speaker, Huang Si-kuan said the Chens usually preferred to listen to the one and one-half hour broadcast, since it was their major source of outside information.

Normally the Chen family ate little meat. Huang Si-kuan could usually feed her entire family for the equivalent of about 60 cents a meal. However she said that four or five times a week, most often at noontime, she prepared a meal with two small meat dishes and a plate of fish, which cost slightly more—just under a dollar in all. (Later, in Hong Kong, we met a young man who had fled from China.[3] He had lived in a village on Kwang Li People's Commune, and his views added

Mealtime in the Chen household. Huang Si-kuan is in the center, in black.

a new perspective to our observations at Kwang Li. For example, he told us that a peasant family like the Chens would more likely enjoy such a hearty meal once a month, *not* several times weekly.)

The Chen family's food budget might seem incredibly low, but food costs consumed a large share of the family's total income. Including profits from sales of their pigs, chickens, and produce from a small family farm plot, in 1972 the Chens' yearly income only came to about $750, plus about 5,700 pounds of unhusked rice. From that amount, Huang Si-kuan would spend $20 to $25 a month for food and daily expenses such as the children's allowances for candy and Ping-Pong balls and paddles, soap, toothbrushes, and the like. (Soap and toothbrushes may be necessities in the West, but they are luxuries in rural Asia.)

Nonetheless, commune officials claimed that many Kwang Li families deposited money in the commune savings bank, which held a total of $445,000 in savings accounts in 1972.

Saving for big purchases was easy on the commune because the peasants were only paid twice a year. Just imagine the "Christmas rush" that followed!

After a payday three years before, the Chen family had spent $60 for a sewing machine, the epitome of prosperity in rural China. The machine, which Huang Si-kuan emphasized "belongs to the whole family," helped them save money: it cost her less than $1.50 to make a blouse for herself and the older girls, and only about 80 cents for material for cotton trousers for her youngest daughter. The Chen matriarch said she made all the clothes for the women and children of her family; but she confessed with a smile that she did not know how to sew men's apparel, so the men in her household had to wear store-bought clothing.

The Chen family also owned a gleaming new bicycle, another status symbol. Bicycles cost about $90. Since there was about one bicycle for every ten persons at Kwang Li, we never saw more than one to a family. Usually the younger members of a household rode the family bicycle.

Commune children contributed to the family welfare, both by participating in collective farming and by tending a private plot of family land. According to Chen family members, young people worked together at such jobs as rethreshing the rice—making certain all the grain was gathered from the stalks. For this kind of work, thirteen-year-old Chen Yung-tsin was paid on the basis of cash and food grain, which

Chen daughter-in-law Tan Wu stitches a child's trousers.

he donated to the family till. Such diligence paid off for the young man. Declared young Chen, "My mother gives me money to buy nearly everything I ask for."

Not all of Chen Yung-tsin's time was devoted to farm labor. During his lunch break from school and on Sundays, he said he liked to swim with the other young people in the village ponds.

The Chen family was affluent by commune standards. Their red brick home consisted of several small, narrow buildings clustered around a tiny stone-stepped courtyard. The main room of their house, a living area with a loft, seemed almost stately compared with some of the cramped, boxlike dwellings just across the village path. Even the food they ate was a notch above average. The fact that Huang Si-kuan retired from the rice fields at age fifty to concentrate on housework proved they could afford to do without the extra source of income she once provided.

Though there was not necessarily any connection between their past stature and their present economic situation, before the CCP came to Sui Kang village, Chen Chi-fun and his family owned a small amount of land which they used for farming. As a result, the Chen family qualified as "middle peasants" in the CCP's official division of rural society according to original class status.

Although conditions varied in China, under one formula used in the 1950 agrarian reform, those pre-Communist families owning over thirty *mou* (five acres) of land were classified as "landlords"; those who owned or rented land from twenty to thirty *mou* (three to five acres) fell into the category of "rich peasants"; families cultivating land from six to twenty *mou* (one to three acres) were "middle peasants"; those whose holdings and tenancies fell below five *mou* (one acre or less) were "poor peasants." Many variations in CCP classification due to family size, type of land use (e.g.,"exploiting" others), and standard of living made assignation difficult, time-consuming, and controversial.

The Chens did not lease land to tenants or hire others to farm it, as "landlords" and "rich peasants" did. Nor did they pay rent to others, like "lower-middle peasants," who owned some, but not all, of their land; "poor peasants," who rented all the land they tilled; or, the lowest on the scale, "farm laborers," who earned their living by manual labor. In pre-Communist China, middle peasants like the Chen family enjoyed relative prosperity and prestige.

The Chens had not lost the distinction of being middle peasants despite the redistribution and collectivization of property rights that equalized landholdings and shattered the rural class system. Even though they were typical members of the people's commune, on the same practical footing as their formerly richer or poorer neighbors, the government continued to stress and preserve their former titles, to remind the peasants of the perpetual class struggle being waged in the countryside. Poor and lower-middle peasants were pitted against rich peasants and "landlord elements" in an enduring ideological war-game.

Although they possessed the same amount of land and were paid on the same basis as their many neighbors, the Chens were still identified as middle peasants. They spoke proudly of their rank, which established them as belonging to a progressive class whose members had always enjoyed favor in the eyes of the CCP.

"We are middle peasants," said Chen-Chi-fun proudly. "We had a better life before 1949, but we did not exploit others.

"Now," he beamed, "we take the poor peasants as our friends."

Chen echoed an often-repeated official party dictum emphasizing unity even among classes with different economic interests:

"The policy here is to rely on the poor and lower-middle peasants and to unite the middle peasants," he said brightly.

But when he recited this familiar maxim, Chen's attitude betrayed a hint of condescension.

The Chen family's categorization as middle peasants had no apparent bearing on their present economic and social status; in fact, Chen Chi-fun and his family may have had to strive slightly harder for success to avoid being penalized for their former prominence.

In contrast to the middle-peasant Chens, their neighbors, Chen Chou, his wife, Lo Chin-loung, and their family belonged to the poor-peasant category. They spoke of their status just as proudly as the middle-peasant Chens, for the poor peasants were the keystone of the new Chinese society and the fountainhead of much political and even cultural inspiration. This poor-peasant family now appeared as well-off as the once more prosperous Chen Chi-fun family. In fact, their new house was even brighter and cheerier than that of their "upper class" neighbors, and all family members appeared to share their pride in it. When asked about their mutual cooperation in housework, Chen

Chou's twenty-two-year-old son Siu-yang replied amusedly, "There's no timetable."

Lo Chin-loung, a slender, soft-spoken peasant woman of forty-eight with prominent teeth and straight, glossy hair pulled back into a neatly braided ponytail, reflected upon the differences between the poverty and insecurity of her youth before 1949, and her middle age in relative prosperity under the auspices of Kwang Li People's Commune.

As she talked, she hunched over a metal laundry basin filled with sudsy water. Soapsuds sloshed over the sides of the shallow tub onto the stone steps of her one-story brick house.

"The greatest change," observed Lo, kneading a foamy collar, "has been in our family's standard of living."

In the old days, she recalled, her family was poor—so poor that they had to rent the land to grow their crops, and they could not afford to repair their dilapidated hundred-year-old house. Each year, after they paid a large share of their crops to the landlord, they needed all the money that remained for basic food and clothing.

In contrast, after communization, as their lives grew more secure and their incomes increased, this family had come to know relative ease. By 1968, after saving for three years, they were able to build a new house next to the old one, for about $750. In 1972, Lo, her husband, and their twenty-two-year-old son earned about $600 and received payment of 3,300 pounds of unhusked rice. They made another $150 from selling three pigs they raised themselves, plus $100 from crops grown on their private plot of land.

These earnings comfortably supported three persons in the Chinese countryside. The poor-peasant Chens' son was married in 1972, but even with an extra mouth to feed, they still spent only about $10 to $15 a month on food and another $3 for such incidentals as soap and toothpaste.

"Of course, we could not afford two extra bicycles," said Lo, "but as for our daily needs, our income is sufficient."

Though his mother carefully measured what she spent of the family income, her daughter-in-law, Hsieh (pronounced *syeh*) Ping, said, "The money is in the house, and we all take what we want."

What if they ran out of money? Hsieh Ping and her husband agreed, laughing, "That would be impossible."

The young couple did aspire to own some luxury items. Though obviously proud of their home and a new bicycle, they said they would like a sewing machine and a watch, neither of which they could afford as yet.

Although the family unit was the pivotal social element in this corner of China, at Kwang Li we found some families who lived permanently apart. Split families represented nothing new to the Chinese people: for countless generations, Chinese husbands have worked far from their homes where salaries were better, sending money home to their wives and children. The first Chinese immigrants to the United States were mostly male; and in Southeast Asia today, split families turn up in all ranks of society, from the journalist who can not afford to bring his family to another city, to the caretaker who bunks near his job and commutes home on weekends.

The CCP did not usually require families to live separately, except in the case of highly educated or skilled couples whose specialties might be needed in separate locations, or when the state could not afford to move a person's family when he or she was transferred.

On the commune, we found examples of both voluntary and assigned separation.

When family members willingly lived apart, it was usually for economic reasons. Such was the case of a grandmother who rested a child on her lap on the doorstep of her home in Sui Kang village. As she talked one steamy morning, she outlined the story of her married life, most of which she had spent alone, while her husband, a railway worker, lived in the town of Shum Chun near the Hong Kong border, a distance by rail and highway of nearly one hundred fifty miles from Kwang Li. Transport in rural China was slow, and travel between the two points required an overnight stop. So this couple only saw each other a few times a year.

This middle-aged woman appeared resigned and accustomed to her fate. But surprisingly, so did Fung Chi-chiang, a twenty-one-year-old construction worker who lived in a dormitory near his work site and saw his wife only on weekends, and a thirty-one-year-old factory employee who traveled to his village in another part of the commune to see his family on Saturdays.

The story of nineteen-year-old Tsin Han-chung, a freckle-faced lathe operator at Kwang Li's small machinery factory, seemed to echo ominously the stories of enforced separation in China that reached the West during the Cold War years. Tsin, who started work near his home on

Nineteen-year-old Tsin Han-Chung, a lathe operator, lives in a dormitory and visits his family in a nearby commune every few weeks.

a nearby people's commune at the age of sixteen, was trained in the skilled task of operating a lathe. Three years later, Kwang Li expanded its machinery factory. Since Kwang Li could not train sufficient qualified workers quickly, the factory administrators recruited about a dozen men from other people's communes. It was at that time that the county labor bureau assigned Tsin to work at Kwang Li. There he lived in a dormitory with the other male factory workers, only returning home every few weeks.

Tsin admitted he missed his friends. "But since coming here," he explained cheerfully, "I have made new friends." He said he and his family did not mind the separation too much, since they could see each other often. If he could not return home, his mother would travel to Kwang Li. Sometimes, when he was alone on his day off, Tsin would ride his bicycle to a nearby resort and restaurant by the side of a mountain waterfall.

This nineteen-year-old member of rural China's industrial corps spent most of his life far from home in an institutional environment. But he considered himself as much a part of his family as ever. He followed the traditional custom of contributing a share of his income to the family treasury. Every month he would give about $5 from his salary of $22 to his family.

3
A NEW CHINESE NATION

Until recently, China was not a nation. It was a collection of villages, many of them separate and insular economic units possessing their own family lineage, ancestor cults, and dialect. Many Chinese peasants never ventured far beyond the walls of their ancestral villages; they barely knew of the existence of other communities just a few miles away.

In the past, the peasants' major intercourse with the outside world was in trading produce and livestock at a nearby market town and rendering rent to landlords and taxes to state authorities. Illiterate and immured by antiquated tradition, man was anchored to his land and woman to her home. The only wanderers were itinerant peddlers and landless laborers who drifted through the countryside eking out their existence.

Surrounding the village clusters, the farm land fanned out, partitioned into tiny, random plots. Since Chinese inheritance laws provided for equal land distribution among male descendants, and since the executors attempted to compensate for the soil's unequal fertility by assigning each survivor land from several different fields, one family's landholdings were often scattered haphazardly in several locations like swatches in a patchwork quilt.

Only a few peasants owned or farmed enough land for their own subsistence. Much of the land belonged to rich peasants or landlords who exacted crippling tribute from their tenants.

Since they functioned as separate, individualized units, few families had the resources to construct elaborate waterworks or irrigation systems, purchase water buffalo, buy insecticide, or hire extra labor during the busy seasons. The peasant families faced the ravages of the elements —periodic drought, flood, and famine—and also disease, crop parasites, and marauding bandits and warlords, alone.

Poverty permeated rural Chinese life, as it still does much of the developing world. In recent centuries, conditions worsened as the country's population grew too large for the cultivable land.

The existence of China's peasants was often miserable and lacking in hope.

The advent of the Chinese Communist Party (CCP) turned rural life in a different direction. After the CCP defeated the ruling Nationalists or *Kuomintang* (KMT) in the civil war of 1946–1949, the Communists converted the bucolic area of Kwang Li and other rural communities like it into a testing ground for one of the most extensive social and economic experiments in history. The new Peking government aimed to create a better life for peasants like Lo Chin-loung and her family —and thus to cement their loyalty to the CCP.

The changes did not occur through a single decree. Instead, step by step, for nearly a decade, the government reorganized rural life, culminating in the eventual formation of the people's communes, and worked to revitalize China's agricultural base, which had been ravaged by centuries of natural disasters and by more than a decade of war.

First, with the proclamation of land reform in the period of 1950–1953, the new government confiscated the land of landlords and rich peasants. This act placed nearly half of China's cultivated land in the hands of formerly landless or land-short peasants and destroyed the landed-gentry class and the clan system.

Subsequently, between 1953 and 1955, mutual-aid teams were established. These were groups of households that pooled their labor and certain draft animals and farm tools, but not their land.

Meanwhile, at Kwang Li, the peasants grappled with their age-old problems.

Like his neighbors in Sui Kang village, the surveyor Chen Chi-fun was still largely dependent for his livelihood upon the fortunes of the weather and water. (Surveying had only provided Chen with part-time employment until 1972, when it became his full-time occupation.) Even after land reform, Chen suffered the ravages of flood, drought, and waterlogged fields.

"From 1953 to 1955," reflected this sallow-faced man somberly, "the mutual-aid teams gave us more manpower so that we could run water wheels, for instance, and teamwork to save the crops from disasters.

"But still, we had bad floods," he remembered.

In the third step, starting about 1955, rural villages were integrated

Chen Chi-fun learned to measure fields in his youth and is now a full-time surveyor.

into agricultural producers' cooperatives (APCs), in which the farmers pooled and jointly managed their land, sharing draft animals and farm tools. Later, by mid-1957, in an "advanced" stage of the APCs (AAPCs), the peasants surrendered all their remaining privately owned land, draft animals, and major farm implements but retained their houses, domestic animals, small-scale tools, and trees.

This represented a drastic undertaking in a society where land was not only the most important form of property, but also the focus of family organization.

Chen Chi-fun remembered that the cooperative organized the peasants and unified their strength to resist natural calamities. But at Kwang Li, this system did not wield sufficient manpower to meet the peasants' agricultural needs and decisively attack their water problem.

In the next episode, the central government decided to form even larger rural communities. What appealed most to China's Communist leaders was the commune, a concept saturated with the legacy of Marxism, conjuring up memories of the Paris Commune, the Russian war communes, and the 1927 Canton Commune.

Even before they seized control, the CCP envisioned that the answer to their country's rural problems lay in collectivization, and the party's founders idealized the militarized, integrated living and laboring system of the commune as the organizational means to achieve this end.

Large-scale communal efforts would permit the recruitment of a massive labor force that could finally conquer such basic problems as water conservation, and communal coordination would increase agricultural production.

The people's communes encompassed more than ten times the size of the AAPCs. (Kwang Li People's Commune embraced what had previously been forty-six AAPCs when it was formed.)

By the end of 1958, some twenty-four thousand people's communes were established. Since they assembled the collective resources and manpower of tens of thousands of individuals, the rural communes were designed to achieve a measure of self-sufficiency previously inconceivable in the countryside. They controlled not only agriculture, but also industry, commerce, education, medicine, the militia, social welfare, public works, and village management.

As conceived in 1958, the people's communes demanded more control than the peasants would accept. The new organization met much opposition primarily because, in an attempt to free women from household labor, the commune leadership had obliged the people to turn over their remaining private land, houses, fruit trees, and other belongings and had begun to establish communal dining halls, nurseries, and even dormitories. In many communes, equal wages for all and, theoretically, free food distribution, resulted in shortages of food.

Encountering opposition to the remote and pervasive authority of the original people's communes, by August 1959 the CCP relegated some administrative authority back to the villages and permitted peasants to keep private plots of land and to receive incentive-based payments.

Further changes came a year later, when village neighborhoods were given virtual control of land, labor, animals, tools, equipment, and the all-important accounting functions. Many larger communes split into smaller-sized, workable units, bringing the national total to approximately seventy-five thousand people's communes.

All these advances and retrenchments caused the economic well-being of Chen Chi-fun and his neighbors to ebb and flow. At last, when the forty-three thousand peasants of the entire market community around Kwang Li town formed a people's commune on October 1, 1958 (not long after the CCP gave communization a formal go-ahead), the peasants assembled sufficient resources to combat floods.

The new commune at Kwang Li mobilized the peasants *en masse* to construct a water conservation system. Working with their bare hands and only one tractor, forty thousand people from Kwang Li and three neighboring communes spent one year building a dam and reservoir in the mountains. It was subsequently linked to an extensive irrigation and drainage network.

As a result, Chen Chi-fun said proudly, "For the past ten years, we have never suffered from floods; and our living standards have improved considerably."

4
NEW ERA AT KWANG LI

On a white cement pillar on the porch of the old schoolhouse that served as Kwang Li People's Commune administrative headquarters, were painted two horizontal red lines—one at shoulder height and another above the eye level of an average Chinese man. The lines were high-water marks. Next to them were written the dates of floods that devastated the surrounding river plain, where most of the population of this commune lived. One mark bore the date 1949, a year bitterly etched in the hearts of all those who remembered when the flood waters from the neighboring mountains combined with the swollen West River to destroy all the crops and take many lives. The floods also demolished dwellings and erased from view many of the graves of the ancestors which rested among the paddy fields.

Opposite the flood record, verses by CCP Chairman Mao were scrawled on the doorposts. They were excerpted from a poem written in 1963, in which Chairman Mao emphasized that while tranquillity reigned in China, the world situation outside its borders was in disorder.

The verses translated: "The four seas are rising, clouds and waters raging" (right side); "The five continents are rocking, wind and thunder roaring!" (left side).

The people of Kwang Li revered these symbols of the present, a time when they insisted they were no longer at the mercy of the elements but firmly in control of their destiny. Yet the past remained to haunt them, in the presence of the high-water marks and in vivid memories.

Formerly floods were the torment of the peasants' existence in this part of Kwangtung Province, as in so many areas of China. Almost yearly, torrents of white water spewed from the mountain passes, flushed across the rice fields, and ripped out the roots of the vulnerable plants, scattering mud and debris.

Drought was equally menacing. It could parch and crack the fertile soil while the farmers' crops withered and died.

The vagaries of wind and weather are no longer as likely to wreak disaster at Kwang Li. Ever since the peasants mustered their collective might to build Kwang Li's thousand-foot dam and its adjacent reservoir, they have mastered the once-destructive forces of nature and harnessed them for productive uses.

When they talked about how they built the dam, the peasants referred to an ancient Chinese folk tale, "The Foolish Old Man Who Moved Mountains." This tale of patience and diligence, rewritten in modern parable form by CCP Chairman Mao, is required reading in the education of every Chinese, to inspire the spirit of perseverence. In the story, an old man is convinced he can move two mountains that are blocking his door. He and his family begin to claw away the huge mountains with their hands. They work relentlessly. When others deride the apparent hopelessness of their project, the old man serenely points to his children, declaring that through generations their unstinting efforts will make the mountains disappear.

So it was at Kwang Li. Together the peasant work force blasted away a mountain. From it they quarried the stone to construct the dam. They anchored the stones with clay from the hills. At the site, they mixed their own cement. With steel supplied by the government, they fashioned pipes to use as conduits for the water. They dug eighteen miles of major drainage canals on the cultivated plain below, as part of a commune-wide network of irrigation ditches that criss-crossed the commune stretching more than two hundred miles, watering 153,000 *mou* (25,500 acres) of land.

After the dam was completed in 1959, the commune had enough water whenever and wherever it was needed for year-round cultivation. Kwang Li's engineers directed the water through several steps. At each stage, the water was used for productive purposes. As a result, local officials claimed that in 1973 they produced ten times as much rice as before 1949.

Behind the dam, a huge man-made reservoir served as a collecting basin, preventing the mountain streams from cascading onto the lowlands. Besides providing reserve water supplies in case of drought, the dam also created a transportation waterway into the remote mountain

View from the top of the dam above Kwang Li's river plain.

areas where roads were unpaved or nonexistent.

The 8½ million gallons of water in Kwang Li's reservoir also drove generators producing 2,000 kilowatts of electricity for Kwang Li and several surrounding people's communes. (One look inside a villager's dimly-lighted home demonstrated how far the commune still had to go by Western standards. But rural electrification, albeit on a small scale, represented enormous progress for China. After dark, much of Southeast Asia today still lives by kerosene lamplight.)

Village organizations paid 7½ cents per hour for electricity, and individual households paid 2½ cents hourly. These contributions provided revenues of about $100,000 yearly to help operate the reservoir and power station. In turn, most of the proceeds from the power station financed further construction.

After the water flowed down from the mountains through a system of aqueducts, generators, and irrigation ditches on the river plain, the commune continued to utilize it. On the edge of the West River, at Kwang Li town, the residents had erected a $100,000 pumping station financed by the government. Inside, six pumps helped to drain excess water from the fields and prevent waterlogging. Three other similar stations were located on the commune.

Traveling beyond the glasslike reservoir on the bumpy dirt road that led back into Kwang Li's pine-covered hills (the "Nine Ditches Mountains"), we could still see work in progress on the conservation project the peasants first undertook in 1958. Working slowly and methodically, using hand labor, the people of the commune were erecting a system of aqueducts and tunnels to channel water from the mountain streams into the ever-expanding hydroelectric power system.

Tying bamboo poles together, workers had woven a lofty web of scaffolding hundreds of feet high. This fragile framework provided the means to construct a reinforced concrete aqueduct that would span the wide gap between two hills. While some workmen clambered in the scaffolding, binding the bamboo shafts together, others below them mixed cement and poured it around steel rods. At the same time, their colleagues were blasting tunnels through the hills.

Eventually rain water and mountain streams would flow through these aqueducts and tunnels and cascade through a series of small generators adding another 1,200 kilowatts of power to the commune's

Above: *Workers tighten bamboo scaffolding for reinforced concrete aqueduct. Using bamboo, which grew nearby, helped cut construction costs.* Below: *One aqueduct already completed.*

total capacity. One day, Kwang Li's leaders even hoped to generate surplus power to sell to other communes.

One Kwang Li resident who was helping to put this plan into action was Fung Chi-chiang, an oval-faced man of twenty-one who erected bamboo scaffolding. Fung declared the "needs of the commune" had motivated him to join the construction work force. Since his home was a mountain village of ethnic minority Hakka people not far from the site of the new aqueduct, Fung said floods were vivid memories for his parents and neighbors. So, he said he accepted the commune's continuing search for better ways to control and utilize water as a personal challenge.

Fung said he had volunteered to leave his job as a farm worker and go to live in the one-room woven bamboo dormitory that sheltered the fifty-odd construction workers. For his high-risk job, rigging the scaffolding, he received about $17 a month, including rice—not much more than he would earn in the fields. He gave the rice to a workers' canteen to be cooked and paid about $6 a month for meat and vegetables.

Because Fung's village was not far from the project, he could return home about six times a month to see his wife, a farm laborer, and his parents.

Fung's job was perilous. He spent about six and a half hours a day tightening bamboo straps around the poles of the scaffold. Fearlessly ignoring the heights, he deftly scrambled amid the forest of stilts. He shaded his custard-colored skin under a wide-brimmed, floppy straw hat.

Fung claimed he was not afraid, since he had worked at such jobs for several years without mishap.

The commune acknowledged the potential danger of working on the scaffold. Fung said he would be paid if he were ill or injured; and should he be permanently disabled, he would be trained for another occupation. Besides, this skilled occupation wielded no small amount of prestige in the remote mountain village Fung called home.

Fung had received only six years of education, yet he claimed his favorite recreation was reading. Asked to name his favorite subject matter, he cited the writings of Marx, Lenin, and Chairman Mao. Those selections may not have seemed like pleasure reading, but they were Fung's only possible choices. Just about the only literature available on the commune was ideological doctrine.

Periodically, farm workers from the commune joined Fung and his colleagues on the construction projects. During the slack farming seasons, commune officials recruited one or two thousand extra workers for large-scale enterprises.

Fung's team also boasted a unique distinction: the only university graduate living on the commune, a water conservation specialist, was assigned to work with them.

The mountain projects were not the only safeguards against floods, for spring rains had not been the only source of flooding in Kwang Li's past. The broad West River had brought commerce to Kwang Li, but it had also wreaked havoc when it overflowed. It was the river, surging over an ancient embankment, that had created the worst flood damage during the 1949 disaster.

After the commune was established, the peasants had moved seventeen million cubic yards of earth, again primarily by hand, to reinforce the old twenty-seven-foot-high embankment. The new dyke stood forty-one feet high and spanned a total width of two hundred ten feet, tapering to a dirt road along the crest. Since its completion in 1959, this embankment had not been breached.

As it had since the first farmers cultivated Chinese soil, the peasants' lifestyle revolved around the rhythm of the seasons. When spring came, the peasants planted rice; at midsummer, they harvested and transplanted; in the golden days of autumn, they collected their second harvest. In the meantime, they tended other crops and performed routine maintenance. Formerly, in the winter, the peasants huddled in their unheated stone huts to endure the cold and dampness. In recent years, the commune organized massive water conservation work to occupy the winter months.

The people of the commune celebrated their new-found freedom from the tyranny of the weather. The opening number of a local propaganda show in a village auditorium was entitled "Spring Comes Early When Men Work Diligently." It was a familiar Cantonese folk melody, given new lyrics to emphasize that by working together, the peasants might master the elements and even, symbolically, hasten the coming of spring.

*　　　　　*　　　　　*

It is doubtful that men can ever change the course of the seasons, but the Chinese Communists were not easily deterred. In Kwang Li, they continued to strive for three rice crops where there were traditionally two; and commune leaders constantly cited Kwang Li's success in controlling its water supply as an inspiration to conquer even greater challenges.

5
ADMINISTRATION

Committees ran most elements of commune government. Since China's Cultural Revolution in the late 1960s, leading committee members were called "responsible persons." Supposedly, this new title sounded more egalitarian than "Assistant-this" or "Officer-in-charge-of-that."

But despite the new nomenclature, the bureaucracy remained essentially the same, and the Chinese understood that. We heard one government interpreter patiently escorting foreign guests to a succession of commune institutions—schools, factories, villages—and introducing a profusion of "responsible persons." At one point, the translator broke his reserve with a smile. From then on, each time he translated the title "responsible person," he would flash a grin.

At Kwang Li as elsewhere in China, day-to-day administrative power was supposed to rest in the hands of a Revolutionary Committee. Theoretically, ideological leadership resided with a Communist Party Committee. But, in reality, both committees tackled the concrete problems of daily life.

Every few weeks, Kwang Li's Revolutionary Committee met in a musty room in the former schoolhouse that accommodated the commune offices. Committee members sat on hard wooden benches at refectory-style tables, under a faded photograph of CCP Chairman Mao. As they drank hot water or tea poured by pigtailed waitresses, the leaders of Kwang Li People's Commune discussed their administrative policies and business.

Originally, this group was known as the administrative committee. But during the Cultural Revolution (roughly 1966–1971), new leadership teams were formed composed of representatives from the commune, the People's Liberation Army, and the CCP. The committees adapted the new name, Revolutionary, along with new duties such as overseeing the efforts of a propaganda team. As the Cultural Revolution subsided, the CCP re-established its own separate Party committee to concentrate on political matters; and the Revolutionary Committee resumed its original administrative functions. Kwang Li residents referred to their commune's administrative group interchangeably as the "administrative" or "Revolutionary" committee.

Throughout China, a similar situation prevailed. But the government at Kwang Li was slightly different from the majority of rural leadership systems. This area was designated as a "model soldier" people's commune. China had many model communes, perhaps thousands, probably at least one in every county. The state singled out these areas for special attention, such as experimental types of fertilizer and mechanical farming aids. Because Kwang Li was one such model area, known for its educational programs, only half, or seventeen, of the thirty-four posts on its Revolutionary Committee were filled by natives of this commune. A higher-level Revolutionary Committee governing Kao Yao county, in which Kwang Li was located, chose the other seventeen from the ranks of government service. These government employees were periodically transferred to other locations.

The county administration thus maintained a tight rein on the local government of Kwang Li, which conveyed directives to the villages and served as a conduit for transmitting the peasants' requests to higher authority.

In addition, another intermediary administrative subdivision called the administrative district supervised several counties. Its officials reported directly to the hierarchy of Kwangtung Province.

Getting to know the personalities who governed Kwang Li proved that Chinese rural authority did not easily fit the image of a monolithic totalitarian state. Far from it; in fact, local politicians wielded considerable influence. The chairman of the Revolutionary Committee and of the local CCP branch was a former army official named Liang Nien, an "outsider" who was born in another part of Kwangtung Province. However, directly beneath him in the hierarchy came a jovial, barrel-chested Kwang Li native named Liang Wei-ming (no relation), who told us he served as the vice-chairman of both the Revolutionary Committee and the CCP Committee on the commune.

Radiating a perpetual toothy grin, with a thatch of black hair shading his bronzed complexion, Liang Wei-ming percolated with enthusiasm. This cheerful administrator, who served as the commune's official host, shattered many myths about Chinese Communist bureaucrats. Little about Liang was reserved or regimented. He exuded hearty energy and a high-spirited enjoyment of life, so much so that he even seemed to relish the administrative details of his office.

As if to destroy any remaining stereotypes about China, Liang, the second highest official on the commune, was constantly breaking into song. He sang many tunes: military songs, folk music, and some melodies he seemed to have improvised himself. Despite the prestige attached to his rank, it seemed perfectly natural to find the uninhibited Liang perched in the branches of a tree, humming a lilting tune as he waited for a political meeting to begin. He accomplished these flights of fancy with no sacrifice of dignity.

Having spent his forty-three years on this commune, where he and his wife were raising their four children, Liang exemplified the stated ideals of Chinese leadership. He was a man of the people who rose through the ranks in his native terrain and apparently held his neighbors' confidence, while attempting to cement their allegiance to CCP authority. He demonstrated a facile command of CCP doctrine and a comprehensive knowledge of commune affairs. At a moment's notice, he rattled off obscure statistics of production and finances, repeating them with his usual verve and *joie de vivre*. He served up all the facts and figures from rice production to the commune's output of peanuts, usually with an appropriate axiom from Chairman Mao (e.g., "Agriculture, forestry, animal husbandry rely upon one another.")

The young man who had fled Kwang Li to Hong Kong provided further perspective about Liang Wei-ming. The illegal emigrant (refugee) noted that the peasants of Kwang Li considered Liang as "okay." (Curiously, this young man insisted Liang did *not* hold a CCP office along with his post on the Revolutionary Committee. Unfortunately, we had no way to resolve this contradiction.)

Since water problems played an integral part in the commune's history, it was not surprising that Liang ascended to political power through water conservation work. In 1964, Liang's achievements in this field earned him a position on the commune administrative committee. During the early stages of the Cultural Revolution, the illegal emigrant in Hong Kong reported, Liang was criticized by his comrades; but he quickly emerged from dishonor. Soon thereafter, in 1968, the new Revolutionary Committee chose Liang Wei-ming as its vice-chairman.

The people of the commune were "consulted" on Liang's appoint-

Exuberant Liang Wei-ming, the second-highest ranking Communist leader on the commune.

ment. And later they had some influence on his promotion.

At a rural political caucus, a list of candidates for the Revolutionary Committee (including Liang), drawn up at county level, was sent for approval to a convocation of village officials and then to a congress of commune members. This local congress or nominating convention consisted of about seven hundred persons, one for every twenty commune residents aged sixteen or over. They submitted their approved list of names to the county Revolutionary Committee, which made the ultimate selection.

Liang Wei-ming had to be "re-elected" about every two years, when the commune members chose another set of delegates to select new Revolutionary Committee members. Again, decisions were subject to approval at higher levels. If the county administrators preferred Liang Wei-ming as vice-chairman, he would most likely retain that position.

Ostensibly, the Revolutionary Committee members had to caucus to choose their leaders. But, said the members, "We don't vote; we reach unanimity."

Political power in China flowed upwards, from the roots of peasant and worker society, and downwards, from the CCP. The state imposed national policies and directives from above. The people wielded minimal influence with the central administration, whose decisions affected their lives.

But this was nothing new in China. In the old society, the masses had virtually no recourse to central authority, and little opportunity to initiate changes in their society. They were often victims of the whims of the local administrators and warlords, as well as of the dictates of landlords and moneylenders. The peasants probably had never had an appreciation of the subtleties of their political milieu, their lives having been dedicated to the problem of survival at its most rudimentary levels.

In view of this lack of political tradition, one important aspect of CCP administration in the people's communes was the selection of some local residents for leadership positions. Even if their political leverage was minimal, the fact that local peasants had any role at all in selecting or even approving their leaders marked important gains for them.

Liang Wei-ming and the other Revolutionary Committee members were known as cadres. So were the other administrative workers (civil servants)—about one thousand in all—who worked in commune government or office jobs. Not every cadre was a member of the CCP, nor were all CCP members considered cadres. Perhaps the best definition of cadres was the simplest: In the words of Vice-Chairman Liang Wei-ming, cadres were "people who belong to offices."

In China, even white collar bureaucrats were supposed to get their hands dirty. In order to refresh and maintain their ties with the peasants, Peking decreed that Revolutionary Committee members and other cadres had to spend at least sixty days each year working in the fields. Each cadre was required to keep a record book certifying the quota was fulfilled.

Directing that administrative cadres work alongside the peasants was one of the many ways the Chinese leadership hoped to ensure that decision-makers would develop policies for the good of the Chinese people as a whole. Required labor forced the cadres to benefit or suffer from their own policies. It was also intended to prevent the isolation of a bureaucratic elite from the reality of arduous physical labor which still typified life in most of China.

Liang Wei-ming's blackened nails and callous-hardened hands and feet testified that he probably did observe this rule. But the illegal emigrant from Kwang Li informed us later that cadres like Liang did not actually till the soil to fill their requirements for field labor. The young man said the cadres would spend their time in the fields performing such jobs as inspecting the dykes to see if they needed patching.

Commune administration was carried out in three tiers, along the lines of ancient, rural practices. When the CCP brought order and discipline to the old rustic way of life, they applied their military terminology to long-established communities. Under the "people's commune" (formerly the market area), they designated farming villages or clusters of villages as "production brigades," and they organized village neighborhoods or small villages into "production teams."

By cleverly utilizing indigenous, functioning organizations in the countryside, the CCP demonstrated a strain of pragmatism. Communist leaders realized they could not disrupt ancient patterns of life without locking horns with stubborn peasant resistance. So they merely gave the existing villages and neighborhoods new revolutionary titles. (Sui Kang village became Sui Kang production brigade, for example.) By acknowledging the peasants' local allegiance and identity, the CCP was better able to maintain order on its own terms in the rural areas.

In Kwang Li (population forty-three thousand), production brigades ranged from about one thousand to five thousand persons each; and production teams generally consisted of three hundred to four hundred residents. Kwang Li had twenty-one production brigades. Nineteen of them were devoted to agriculture, one to transportation, and another to fishing enterprises. There were about two hundred thirty production teams on this commune.

These three units forming the core of Chinese country life—the people's commune, the production brigade, and the production team—functioned both together and independently. The production team exerted the strongest influence over the peasants' lives.[4]

Each of the three groups collectively controlled such assets as farm land, forests, water and water resources, tools, machinery, draft animals, factories, and mines; all of which the three units might share, rent to each other, or own separately. The commune also owned the farm land at Kwang Li, which it leased to the production brigades and production teams for a period of thirty years.

The commune administration was supposed to oversee operations that served the commune as a whole, depended upon the aggregate skills of all the residents, were too big or too complex for the smaller villages to undertake or which drew on the natural resources of the entire people's commune.

For instance, the villages maintained small fish-ponds, scattered through the emerald paddy fields. But harvesting the daily catch where the irrigation canals dumped into the West River required so much labor that the commune assigned this task to its fishery production brigade.

Where the canal water poured into the river, the fishery workers had constructed an elaborate bamboo fish trap to collect fresh-water fish that had spawned and grown to maturity in Kwang Li's more than two hundred miles of irrigation channels.

Within the bamboo barrier, fishery workers in undershirts and shorts splashed barefoot in water up to their shoulders, brandishing nets as they drove the fish to shore. Just one attempt yielded an impressive catch, with many ten-, twelve-, and even fifteen-pounders flopping ashore.

In one year, commune officials reported that these workers had trapped about forty thousand pounds of fresh-water fish. Whenever possible, the commune capitalized on its natural resources. A purchasing station marketed these fish on the commune for about 20 cents a pound, to help pay Kwang Li's operating costs.

Among its many functions, the commune leadership was responsible for disaster or flood relief and was entrusted with the personal welfare of its citizens.

Kwang Li's welfare system—or its absence—provided an example of the CCP's pragmatic approach to rural administration.

Aside from paying minimal fees for medical care, most peasant farmers lived their lives untouched by the commune's welfare program. In lieu of public assistance, the government relied on ancient custom, with families caring for their less fortunate members. In their old age, most peasants were supported by their children, as most elderly Asians are to this day.

This practice might not seem in keeping with the ideal of a socialist welfare state, but the CCP took advantage of tradition to save money and avoid a complicated social security system.

Since children traditionally provided for their parents as they grew old, the agricultural workers received no specific retirement benefits. But the production teams assured all elderly citizens who had no children of food, clothing, housing, medical care, and a funeral. These people's possessions would revert to the collective ownership of their neighbors after their death.

Despite the social pressure in the old society to marry and bear offspring to serve as their future guarantors, some peasants never married. Some men simply could not raise the money to buy a bride. From ancient times until 1949, the childless or unmarried, or those couples whose children and relatives perished from disease and famine, had been left to fend for themselves in their old age.

Thus children, especially sons, who were bound by the cult of ancestor-worship to support their parents, were more than mere status symbols of a successful marriage. They were the only form of insurance available to the peasants. So it was logical and necessary for parents to desire and bear many offspring.

In much of Asia today, dependence on the family still constitutes the only reliable form of security, and young couples are encouraged to bear many sons in order to provide for their old age. So China's "fall-back" old-age care system represented a breakthrough. And by reducing the need for large families, the Chinese system may have contributed to the apparent success of the country's population control.

Before communization, old age might have been a painful experience for one of Kwang Li's elderly bachelors, sixty-one-year-old Hsieh Shi-kuei. Without children to care for him, he might literally have perished.

"I had a very bitter life before 1949," mused Hsieh, his wizened face puckering as he drew deeply upon a home-rolled cigarette in the shade of a village bamboo grove. "I was very poor, so poor that I had to leave this region and work as a coolie in Canton."

Hsieh had always enjoyed caring for chickens in his spare time; so in 1969, when he grew too old to work in the fields, his production brigade assigned him to a "side-line occupation," tending a flock of chickens. The profits from selling eggs and meat helped to support a village bamboo factory adjacent to Hsieh's chicken coop. This income also enabled Hsieh to earn more money in his old age than he used to make when he was younger.

It was no wonder that Hsieh asserted, "Life is improved because we are liberated, because Chairman Mao leads us in the correct way."

Hsieh's comments on his personal happiness revealed candidly how things had changed since the days when elderly persons had to take any work they could find, merely to survive.

"If I didn't like this job," he noted wryly, indicating his relative freedom of choice, "I wouldn't be here."

6
COMMERCE AND FINANCE: STRIVING FOR SELF-SUFFICIENCY

Even in the controlled economy of the People's Republic of China, the manager of the largest general store in Kwang Li said the commune added a standard mark-up of about 10 percent on all retail items.

Nevertheless, prices were low, and the government kept them that way. In this store, peasants could purchase a bar of soap for 15 cents, four-by-six-foot blankets for $14, cigarettes for 10 to 15 cents a pack, razor blades for 75 cents a package, a small bottle of rice wine for $1.10, a basketball for about $4, and air pressure lanterns for $18.50.

Once, Kwang Li town had been a flourishing river community, bustling with shops and vendors. Now only a river-front street of blank, shuttered store fronts provided testimony to the town's past. Ironically, the name Kwang Li translates literally as "wide open for business."

The town had served as the commune's commercial center. Today, the commune administration supervised the few dozen remaining businesses. Small shops and street peddlers were consolidated into "collective stores"—dimly lighted one-room enterprises, open to the street, that displayed a small array of goods such as toys, dried vegetables, wine, and cigarettes.

Most of the commerce was transacted in the state-run general store.

Like the company store in a company town, the general store did a thriving business, admonished by a CCP slogan in bold, red Chinese characters: "Serve the people!" Most of the wares were referred to as "daily-use articles"—a sturdy-looking but not particularly enticing assortment of flashlights, pocket knives, toothbrushes, plastic combs, cooking utensils, soap dishes and the like. There were a few frivolous

A sporting goods and stationery store in Kwang Li town.

items. A simple array of small rubber squeak-toys in the shapes of colorful animals mesmerized the younger children.

One prestige item, a treadle-operated sewing machine, was available in two models, the $63 "Canton" and the $75 "Shanghai." The store manager reported he sold a total of one hundred twenty of them in 1972.

A typical shopper, twenty-two-year-old Ho Wei-chun, bought a $60 wrist watch for what seemed to be a worthy purpose in proletarian China: "to tell what time to go to work."

Ho worked at the commune's starch factory. Her salary of $22.50 a month measured among the highest for young people on the commune, since her job required a high degree of technical skill in this rural community.

Shopping for the watch was a special occasion, because it took Ho six months to save for it. So she brought along two girl friends to help her choose.

She made her selection from among several models for perhaps the most universal of all feminine reasons.

"It's prettier," she said of the final choice.

Profits from the store's 10 percent mark-up helped the commune administration to support itself and to pay the salaries of manager Li Sun-an and his clerks. Their pay checks ranked above the average commune salaries but below those of some factory workers. Li earned $22.50 a month including food grain (rice).

Manager Li described how the commune practiced a rural Chinese form of market research.

"We have found what people want, through experience. We also enlist the poor peasants' opinions about what is good and not good."

The manager said that the commune financial and trade administration office, which ran the store, placed orders for goods with the county headquarters. The commune office requested about 80 percent of the merchandise at least three months in advance. It was possible, said manager Li, to requisition some smaller items of the daily-use category on five days' notice; and commune staff members could go to the county seat to immediately procure items in high demand. But the store manager intimated that the staff rarely went to these extremes.

Just down the street from the general store were the offices of the commune's supply and marketing cooperative (SMC), which ran all mercantile operations on the commune. The SMCs were supposed to procure industrial and farm products from the rural areas for the cities, and to supply the countryside with clothing, consumer goods, subsidiary foodstuffs, tools, cattle, fertilizer, and insecticides.

Kwang Li's 370 SMC employees operated a cooperative store in the commune center with branches in each production brigade, and they controlled the stores on the main street of Kwang Li town. There were also a pharmacy, a barber shop, a tailor, and several restaurants in the town.

SMC agents also traveled to the commune's nearly inaccessible mountain villages to buy goods and handicrafts made by the villagers, who were minority Hakkas, and to sell consumer supplies to them. In these remote areas, where transportation was difficult, the SMC extracted a 3 percent commission and purchased virtually all the peasants' products.

In order to meet some of the operating costs of the commune, the administration at Kwang Li operated seventeen revenue-producing services, including an agricultural machinery factory and repair shop, a factory producing edible and industrial starch, a rice mill, two peanut oil processing plants, a winery, a cork and vacuum flask insulation factory, the tailor shop, and a civil engineering team. Vice-Chairman Liang Wei-ming noted that few if any of these operations existed before the CCP took over in 1949, or even before the commune was formed in 1958. According to Liang, the combined 1972 income from these enterprises amounted to (U.S.) $1,085,000, yielding a gross profit of $240,000 and a net profit of $110,000. As one example, a factory turning out wooden agricultural implements grossed $140,000 and netted $16,000.

These figures constituted formidable sums on the commune, where costly expenditures were few. The absence of rents and low labor charges contributed to low overhead. Also, the CCP exhorted the peasants to make the most efficient use of the resources available to them.

A commune fish hatchery (called a "fish fry" by our interpreters, who had acquired this term from British usage) was a vivid implementation of this CCP guideline.

Next to a series of shallow fish-breeding ponds, excavated amid low-lying paddy land, stood a brick pigsty. In an elemental, round-robin recycling process, the fish and the pigs supported each other.

Fodder from nearby vegetable plots provided food for the pigs. The pigs' droppings, in turn, nourished the fish. The fish yielded excrement which fishery workers scraped off the bottom of the ponds for fertilizer in the original vegetable gardens. Workers repeated a disinfecting process several times to ensure that natural fertilizer (feces) contained no disease organisms. And so the cycle continued.

Besides being economical, the fish hatchery was also lucrative. Commune officials reported that in 1972, this station sold some 32,000 *catties* (about 35,000 pounds) of large fish and some 2.5 million catties of smaller varieties.

The fish hatchery operation, and the fact that it was profitable, showed how Kwang Li's officials pursued another of the goals set forth by Chairman Mao: self-sufficiency.

Ideally each people's commune aspired to become a self-sustaining unit. Then, in case of national calamity, disaster, or war, a commune could survive independently. Such a system did not encourage the most efficient usage of manpower and resources. But theoretically it could guarantee China's survival as long as the country remained a basically peasant, agrarian society.

This attempt to create self-sufficient communes may have been related to China's overall defense strategy. Composing a nation of independent units minimized the possibility that a limited number of nuclear strikes could render China defenseless and vulnerable to economic collapse. In ground warfare, too, since each commune could theoretically survive without outside support, an invading army could capture large segments of territory without necessarily affecting adjacent areas.

Another reason the people's commune administration engaged in so many lucrative activities was that the commune did not collect any local taxes. However, the Kwang Li administration was required to pay taxes to the state. A total income tax payment of $19,000 in 1972 represented about 17 percent of the net intake from the commune enterprises in that year.

Kwang Li paid a state sales tax, ranging from 1.5 to 1.8 percent, depending upon the product. The government granted tax exemptions to profits from the commune's agricultural machinery and wooden tools factories, in order to promote production there. Taxes were also levied on the sale of surplus rice (which accounted for most of the commune's taxes) and on certain other crops such as hemp and sugar.

7
PRODUCTION BRIGADES (VILLAGES)

"I have a strong feeling for my family," declared Lo Chin-loung, the forty-eight-year-old peasant woman who lived in Kwang Li's Sui Kang production brigade.

"But I also have a strong feeling for the production brigade," she said. "Without the production brigade, I would not have this family."

Beneath the headquarters staff of the people's commune in the organizational hierarchy came the production brigade. These brigades were composed of large villages or groups of small villages. (Members of the fishing and transportation production brigades were recruited from a wider area.)

Production brigade officials dealt with the important questions of crop allotments, production targets, and the technical means—such as soil conservation—to achieve these ends. In Kwang Li, the production brigades also ran the schools and supervised politics, medicine, and recreation. The brigades also served as administrative intermediaries, wedged between the people's commune staff and the all-important neighborhood production teams in the organizational table.

An administrative (steering) committee of peasants managed each production brigade. Elected or re-elected every three years by approval of the peasants, this committee coordinated official village activities.

In Sui Kang production brigade, an ancient settlement of brick dwellings set among tranquil ponds in Kwang Li's verdant valley, committee members met about once a week, often at the edge of a paddy field at twilight. Usually, said one member, they discussed "how to improve production . . . to have a bumper crop"; and they drafted detailed plans to ensure a good harvest. "We have free discussion and express different

Lo Chin-loung attributed her family's rising income to the production brigade.

opinions," said this official. But ultimately, in characteristic Chinese bureaucratic fashion, he reported: "We reach unanimity."

At one late afternoon session, the nine administrative committee members of this production brigade squatted or sat cross-legged in a circle on the dry grass bordering a paddy field. Still wearing their work clothes, they appeared relaxed. Some smoked, others laughed among themselves. One woman with a leathery face chewed pensively on a blade of tall grass.

This meeting was convened at the height of the growing season, so the discussion topics—rice-eating insects and waterlogging—were of crucial importance. To demonstrate the urgency of the insect threat, the vice-chairman, a peasant farmer who appeared no more or less ostentatious than his comrades in his simple country apparel, had brought along one of the tiny culprits, a caterpillar-like insect that he displayed in his cupped palm.

Acting upon members' suggestions, the committee moved to counteract the insect challenge by setting lures—lamps set above pools of insecticide—and by spraying pest-killer in larger quantities than usual. The committee also proposed a third solution, a traditional method that only a country with China's vast population could conceive of: hundreds of peasants would comb the rice fields looking for insect-bitten stalks. The peasants would remove the offenders by hand, plucking the tiny insects from the plants one by one!

During the committee's term of office, each member was assigned special responsibilities. Chairman of the group since 1958 was CCP member Ma Ping-kuan, a fifty-three-year-old native of Sui Kang village who came from a poor peasant family. Ma, who had attended school for only three years, said he had taught himself to read enough characters to understand books and the newspaper.

This easygoing peasant official spoke of politics and revolution through personal experience. During the early 1940s, the young Ma had left the poverty of his native village to apprentice as a shoemaker in Canton. But, he told us, he could not make enough money to feed himself in the city, so he had returned to Sui Kang village a year later. In 1953, Ma had assumed leadership of the ten families in his mutual-aid team, the scheme under which peasants pooled their labor but not their land. The following year, he had joined the CCP; and in 1958, he had risen to the leadership of the production brigade. Ma must have been a CCP faithful, for of all the Kwang Li bureaucrats we met, he alone had traveled to Peking. Yet his salary, based on his farm labor, did not exceed that of his fellow workers.

The administrative committee included:

Male:

Hong Kuei-fun, vice-chairman, in charge of "side-line" occupations (tasks other than the main agricultural preoccupations);

Chan Fook-yuen, the party secretary of the production brigade's CCP branch;

Wu Pan-ti, vice-secretary of the CCP branch;

Tan Fu-ti, who was in charge of public security (police work).

Female:

Hsieh Sai-ying, who directed women's work and was the chairman of the production brigade women's committee;

Hsiu San-san, who was in charge of women's work;

Li Kuei-chun, who was in charge of youth work, vice-chairman of the women's committee and vice-secretary of the CCP Youth League branch in the brigade. Undoubtedly one of the most beautiful women we saw in China, Li tossed her long plait of hair across her shoulders as she concentrated on the meeting;

Ho Chih, committee member.

Several times each year, the Sui Kang administrative committee convened a mass meeting of all the thirty-eight hundred residents of the production brigade in a spacious, spartan auditorium opposite the village school. Inside the auditorium entrance hall, a huge, painted mural depicting Chairman Mao informally attired, casually smoking a cigarette against a backdrop of mountain scenery, greeted the villagers. During these brigade meetings, the peasants crowded onto the long wooden benches in the main hall and participated in discussions of the annual production plan, work assignments, and other village business.

Like the people's commune administration, the production brigade leaders also ran their own set of income-generating enterprises to cover administrative expenses.

Sui Kang production brigade's administrators operated a bamboo factory; a rice mill and peanut oil processing factory; a wooden tools factory; a transportation team; tractor and agricultural machinery repair stations; farms for pigs, cows, and chickens; a forestry station; and a water pumping and hydroelectric power station.

These facilities yielded a gross income slightly under $500,000 in 1972, which, when costs were deducted, netted a brigade income of about $310,000. Peasants from other areas of the commune recognized Sui Kang as one of the most prosperous production brigades at Kwang Li, the young illegal emigrant later informed us in our Hong Kong interviews.

Under commune supervision, the production brigade administered the agricultural production of its production team subdivisions. Production brigades such as Sui Kang also developed and maintained water conservation and capital construction projects, in conjunction with commune-wide plans.

Civil affairs also fell under production brigade jurisdiction. This area of responsibilities included construction of homes; the militia; culture and recreation; education, which usually meant operating primary and junior middle schools (providing the first seven years of formal education); and public health, which was maintained through a brigade clinic complete with midwives. Political instructions were disseminated through the production brigade leadership to the production teams.

Like the people's commune administration, the production brigade provided commercial services such as a general store. Here, villagers could purchase a variety of household items, from cloth and dishes to pork and sausages processed on the commune.

Customers in Sui Kang production brigade's cooperative store could buy a ladleful of soy sauce for about 15 cents, cloth for $1.50 a yard, sun-dried preserved vegetables (since there was no refrigeration in rural China) for only 6½ cents a pound, and even a bicycle for $90.

In every way possible, commune members attempted to utilize indigenous natural products and by-products.

Sui Kang production brigade's one-room bamboo factory turned out a variety of items including hats, fertilizer scoops, and many types of baskets for farm work. Brigade workers collected bamboo leaves for fertilizer and fuel. Every year, some $65,000 from sales of 3.2 million *catties* (about 3.5 million pounds) of bamboo accumulated in the brigade accounts.

Previously bamboo grew only in the mountains, several miles away. But, starting in 1964, the peasants of Sui Kang village began cultivating this delicate plant in the valley near their homes. Transplanting demanded skillful selection of proper strains and careful cultivation, but the villagers wanted easier access to the useful bamboo shoots.

After they had grown enough bamboo to start producing articles, the production brigade purchased two bamboo slicing machines from the

Everything from cloth and dishes to pork and sausages: Sui Kang production brigade general store.

commune's agricultural machinery supply station at a total cost of $135. Inside the simple bamboo factory, one man and one woman operated these whirring machines, slicing the hard stalks into narrow, flexible strips. Above on the wall was painted the CCP slogan, "Take food grain as the key link and make all-round development." Nearby, a dozen coworkers sat on the packed dirt floor, weaving and binding baskets, scoops, and other farm implements.

The people of this village enjoyed security unprecedented in Chinese history. Professor C. K. Yang, a sociologist from the University of Pittsburgh who is the author of a well-known book on Chinese family and village life, has pointed out that the establishment of order and the eradication of banditry constituted one of the major changes in China since 1949. Professor Yang, who returned to China in 1972 for the first time in two decades, believes the new sense of security is one of the CCP government's greatest accomplishments.[5]

As she wrung a faded blue shirt, bending over her laundry tub, Lo Chin-loung offered testimony to Professor Yang's observation:

"I feel very safe," she said. "Under the leadership of the people's commune, I don't think anyone can make trouble."

As commonplace as this may seem in the West, in China such serenity is revolutionary.

But, paradoxically, Kwang Li and other people's communes like it devoted considerable efforts to protecting themselves against a distressing variety of threats, real or imagined.

Public security (police work) was a vital function of the production brigade, and Tan Fu-ti, the committee member in charge of security for Sui Kang village, was one of the brigade's most important officials.

Though Tan told us the people's militia patrolled their villages unarmed, we saw evidence of security precautions on the commune. Office drawers were padlocked and windows were barred. Our driver insisted on locking our minibus whenever he was out of sight.

Since 1949, the CCP has taken great pains to persuade the peasants to defend themselves against "class enemies," and Tan Fu-ti insisted that this was his biggest responsibility.

"Class enemies" were the new demons of China. This generic pejorative encompassed those elements of society that, in the CCP belief, represented threats to China's proletarian revolution. In Kwang Li, "class enemies" usually referred to dispossessed landlords whose prop-

Bamboo stalks converted into pliable strips for weaving.

erty had been redistributed among the peasants in the early 1950s. The landlords now worked on the same basis as any peasants, tilling the soil side by side with their former tenants, distinguished only by the memory of their past prosperity. But this stigma was something the CCP would not forgive and forget.

The magnitude of any threat to security did not seem very formidable. According to security officer Tan, there had not been a murder on the commune for over twenty years, and the worst crimes were petty larcenies. The most recent crime he could recall was committed by a former landlord. This "class enemy" allegedly stole produce from another peasant. His punishment was to return the stolen goods.

Justice appeared to have a double standard at Kwang Li. If the culprit were a simple peasant, Tan stated that he or she would probably be "re-educated" by the security committee, with a private dressing down. If the peasant's crime were serious, such as a major theft, he or she might have to undergo public self criticism before several peers. But if a former landlord were apprehended for misdemeanors, the "class enemy" might be subjected to the humiliation of a "struggle meeting" before the entire production brigade.

According to several residents, one such struggle meeting was staged in Sui Kang auditorium in 1972. One thousand peasants looked on as a former landlord was criticized for "serious crimes." He was charged with publicly carping that private property was better than collective ownership, and he was accused of attempting to barter one of his nieces in marriage. His penalty: working under the supervision of the poor peasants, which was essentially what he was already doing.

Security officer Tan Fu-ti said that if this exercise did not achieve results, an offender might be sent to the county court, where he or she might face a prison term.

Whenever the CCP went hunting for class enemies, the former landlords headed the list.

They were the scapegoats of the commune. The illegal emigrant in Hong Kong stated that former landlords' children could not advance beyond primary school, and their sons had difficulty marrying daughters of peasant families.

There was virtually no possibility the former landlords could pose any serious threat to the commune more than two decades after they had been reduced to *de facto* peasant status. Yet the second son of surveyor Chen Chi-fun revealed he had been taught that the landlords' alleged criticism of CCP rule constituted real danger.

"The rumors [generated by the landlord] damage relations between members of the commune," said twenty-one year-old Chen Yung-tien, a field worker. And that, Chen insisted, posed a security risk.

Neither young Chen nor his father could offer convincing evidence to substantiate the belief that the landlord's criticism could directly harm the commune system.

In fact, Chen's father said he did not believe peasants would ever accept the landlords' capitalistic notions.

"Most of the peasants love the commune," he said with conviction. "It is impossible for them to have thoughts against it."

"Were there any good landlords?" we asked.

The younger Chen, perhaps more liberal in outlook than his father, cited a landlord in his production team who wanted to "return to capitalism."

"If the landlord elements have been re-educated very well," the young man allowed, "they can change."

But the elder Chen was still eager to echo the party line and to condemn the landlords as a class.

"All the landlords exploited the people," he retorted. "If they were fair, then they were not landlords."

8
PRODUCTION TEAMS (NEIGHBORHOODS)

Standing side by side, the old and new houses of Lo Chin-loung's family graphically illustrated the contrasts between the old China and the new China that had developed here since Kwang Li People's Commune was formed. The soot-blackened, windowless room of the hundred-year-old house, with its brick wood-burning stove, belonged to the Middle Ages. Built in 1968, the new house adjacent to it was spacious, airy, and cheerful, with many windows and an open loft letting sunlight filter onto the stone floor.

The new house represented the best kind of family dwelling to be found on the commune. But such houses were available to families who consolidated their efforts and saved their incomes.

Throughout Kwang Li, houses were clustered in village neighborhoods, aligned along narrow dirt paths that led to the surrounding paddy fields. These neighborhoods were divided into production teams, the grass-roots ownership and labor units of the commune which handled basic production, accounting, and payment. Daily work, political instruction, and even leisure-time revolved around these neighborhood teams.

Production teams varied widely in size at Kwang Li, but they usually corresponded to a natural, often traditional grouping of families that had functioned together long before the idea of people's communes originated. Across Kwang Li's irrigated plain were scattered larger villages of several thousand persons, each the size of a workable production brigade. Most of Kwang Li's population lived in the villages of the river plain. These large village brigades were subdivided into production teams consisting of about three hundred or four hundred residents. But in the rugged mountains overlooking the rice-growing plain, the village populations were much smaller—several hundred people, or about the same size as the lowland teams. Accordingly, entire mountain villages were designated as production teams, and the far-flung collection of mountain teams was classified as one production brigade.

In many parts of China, the production teams roughly corresponded to the former clans or extended families, which had composed entire villages. Contemporary Chinese propaganda proudly proclaimed the demise of the clan, with its allegiances, nepotism, and interclan rivalry. The nuclear family, however, had been preserved.

Clan structure had virtually disappeared at Kwang Li. The only remaining trace of the clans that used to regulate life in Lo Chin-loung's village was the shell of an ancestral temple which the peasants now used as a granary. Here, before 1949, many clans had existed within single villages. Rural leaders at Kwang Li stressed that nowadays the production teams did not follow former clan lines. Instead, the teams duplicated the membership of the old mutual-aid teams of the early 1950s.

Production team activities had a much more direct effect on the daily lives of the peasants than the people's commune or production brigade. The team implemented crop production, distribution, and remuneration; and team workers were solely responsible for their own profits and losses.

In each neighborhood, six to eight production team leaders, two or three of whom were usually CCP members, handled political-ideological functions, assigned jobs and payment scales, and were responsible for finance, production, women's work, the militia, and other administrative duties.

Within the team, individual peasants exercised their greatest input into the leadership process. However, commune and brigade leaders had the authority to override team-level decisions.

For instance, in one incident involving premarital sex, the members of a Kwang Li production team opposed the decision of the team's administrative committee, calling it unfair. The former Kwang Li resident who had fled to Hong Kong reported this incident concerning his neighbors. He said the production team leaders publicly denounced the young man involved, "locked him up" for one week, and took away his job. This action created an atmosphere so unpleasant for the young woman, who was pregnant, that she underwent an abortion. The emigrant in Hong Kong said the couple's team neighbors protested the harsh treatment the man received and recommended that the woman should share some of the man's blame. But the brigade upheld the team's actions and the young man's disgrace.

Even at team level, self-sufficiency was promoted as an important goal. The production teams controlled the land, forests, and water within their jurisdiction;[6] and they enjoyed prime rights to their own draft animals, farm tools, small machinery and, most important, labor. The people's commune and the production brigades could not requisition peasant labor without compensation to the production teams in the form of money or services.

In 1961, the commune administration officially assigned the land at Kwang Li to the production brigades. The brigades in turn delegated their share to the production teams, with the promise that the assignments would not change for a period of thirty years. Since then, the peasants have farmed their assigned land communally, with each team member receiving a proportionate share of the produce and its profits at harvest time.

Under the direction of the production team leaders, the team members considered and ultimately implemented annual production plans for the communal land. Each year, as part of a nationwide program, these plans designated how this team land would be farmed, specifying every detail down to the type of crops to be grown and the exact allocation of each parcel of earth during each season.

These production plans were drawn up through a bureaucratic system of descent and ascent.

At high levels of government, officials projected the quality and quantity of production they desired from the Chinese countryside each year. They transmitted their intentions through the provinces down to the county, commune, and production brigade levels. The brigade leaders added their expectations and handed the revised plans to the production teams.

Kwang Li's production teams usually got their first look at the tentative proposals for the following year's schedule about the first week of December. The four hundred members of Lo Chin-loung's production team would spend the first part of December discussing the suggested plan. They could make their own recommendations to be endorsed at a general team meeting.

Then, in turn, the production team would submit its revised plan back up the line to production brigade authorities. By the end of December, after the plan had bounced back and forth between production brigade and production team administrations, perhaps several times, the brigade would have developed a final, specific plan for the coming year.

Considerable controversy centered around this annual decision-making ritual. At the provincial and county level, agricultural officials were known to compete with each other, each striving to make the highest pledge for the coming year's production. For example, one county leader might vow that the people of his area would contribute a certain amount of rice to the national supply. Then another official might pledge even more rice from his domain. However, their promises might backfire if they made unrealistic demands upon the people who would have to produce the projected amounts!

Nevertheless, higher-level officials seemed to appreciate the vital role that the teams played, since the production teams were the fundamental interface between man and the soil at the bottom of the extended chain of command. The production teams were allowed some autonomy in hammering out the final plans, probably so that the teams would identify with them. This technique demonstrated the CCP's sensitivity—or acquiescence—to human nature.

The production teams also debated which crops to cultivate, although their discussions were often mere verbal exercises, since the peasants had to fulfill national targets in the production of some crops, such as rice. The team members might prefer to grow cash crops such as vegetables; but inevitably, under pressure from the authorities, the teams would "decide" to grow rice.

Such considerations were vital, because the teams also strove to increase their production and to guarantee the peasants a "raise" every year.

In four or five years, the value of a day's work at average tasks had risen from about 30 to 44 cents for the members of one Kwang Li production team.

Increased wages assumed great significance, because China's controlled economy was protected from inflation, and the government maintained prices for consumer goods at stable levels.

Production team members also decided how to allocate their annual budgets. The budgets were planned within the limits of state-imposed quotas. But within a given year the production teams were permitted certain leeway. Expenses were usually allocated for reserve supplies, welfare funds, and future investments. Welfare expenditures included insurance and collective services such as infant and child care facilities, canteens for field workers during the busy seasons, subsidies for elderly persons with no familial means of support, and cooperative medical care.

Production teams could make adjustments in each category. For example, official procedure dictated that teams could allocate between 5 and 8 percent of their funds for reserves, between 2 and 3 percent for welfare, and between 3 and 5 percent for future production. They could shift priorities from one area to another within these flexible boundaries, but their decisions were subject to review at brigade level.

Team leaders said they tried to adjust quotas so that every year they could distribute a slightly greater amount of money to workers than the year before. But this was an ideal, and in practice it was not always possible to meet this goal if the collective harvest suffered a decline.

When the people's communes were established, opportunities for individual initiative and private enterprise had been severely limited. But the CCP did permit each family to retain one private plot of land to grow its own produce. Each production team was supposed to set aside approximately 5 percent of its land for private plots, which were allocated according to family size. These plots were tiny parcels of land, comparable in size to backyard gardens in the West. Adult laborers were entitled to 0.1 *mou* (1/60 of an acre) of land, while children received half that amount. A family's aggregate, known as their private reserve land plot, belonged to the whole family, who cultivated it together.

The peasants were free to choose what crops to grow, but commune leaders were quick to remind visitors that the cultivation was for fodder and family use—not for commercial purposes. The only exceptions were taro and yam crops, which the local SMC (supply and marketing cooperative) purchased and transported in bulk to city consumers.

The existence of these private plots represented a radical departure from earlier CCP practices. The story of how the family of production brigade surveyor Chen Chi-fun gained, lost, and then regained possession of private land demonstrated how the various stages of collectivization affected the peasants on this commune.

"Before Liberation," Chen Chi-fun began, referring to the era before the CCP takeover, "we had about three *mou* [about half an acre] of land. We cultivated it ourselves. First I worked in a match factory and then as a salesman, so we were always self-sufficient." Chen's family was among the minority of peasants in those days who owned their own land. (Later, when the new reverse status system developed under CCP leadership, Chen and his family were thankful they had not rented out land.)

Chen recalled that the coming of the Japanese in the 1930s and the civil war that followed had barely affected his village. But when the CCP introduced land reform in the early 1950s, the Chen family had felt the first stirrings of the wind that was to sweep through every corner of China. Although decrees deprived them of the prestige of being landowners, at first the CCP had left the Chens with more property— their previous allotment plus an additional grant, totalling five *mou,* or five-sixths of an acre.

After land reform, practically all the land had continued under private cultivation. Then, in a drastic step, when the people's communes were established, the fields were declared to be the property of all citizens of the commune. Chen Chi-fun had to give up all his land, both the new possessions and his previous holdings, to commune proprietorship.

But this measure had proved too revolutionary, and about eight months later, 5 percent of the collective land had been designated for private plots. The final transaction left the Chens with .106 of an acre, six short furrows of land—12 percent of their former possessions. On their family plot, just a short walk from their home, they raised yams, peanuts, ginger, green melons, and taro to feed their pigs. This produce provided a small supplement to the Chens' income from their jobs in the production brigade fields and industries. But their vegetables helped feed the family, and the meticulous care most plots received indicated they were appreciated.

Not all members of their production brigade selected which crops they would grow, with a balanced diet in mind. It was a rare family that did not devote at least part of its private plot to growing tobacco for "roll-your-own" cigarettes, which the commune-dwellers puffed constantly. Even some teachers in the village school laughingly admitted they raised tobacco. Hsieh Shi-kuei, our chicken-farmer friend, devoted all his private plot to tobacco, so profound was his interest in smoking. As a result, on a sunny day, curly greenish-brown tobacco would be drying on racks on the doorsteps of just about every house in the village.

The production teams assigned private plots to their members equitably. Since the land itself was not uniformly fertile, in the early days there had been some disputes in Chen Chi-fun's production brigade (Sui Kang). So the peasants had decided to rotate the location of their private plots every year. According to production brigade leader Ma Ping-kuan, this practice was not new to the people of his village, who had rotated their crops "even before Liberation," to improve the condition of the soil. In this commune, though, he added that a choice between two private plot systems—rotation and permanent tenancy—depended on the whims of individual production teams.

Although the original percentage of private land allocated since communization was unchanged, the amount of land available for family plots had increased. The population had grown, and more land had become available for cultivation, thanks to continuing efforts to reclaim the mountain terrain for farming.

Besides land, the state respected other private possessions, such as incomes, bank savings, household goods, and domestic animals. The consumption and sale of fish and fowl was unrestricted; but since pork was a precious commodity, the state forbade the private sale of pigs except for breeding purposes. Pork, sugar, fresh and salted fish, cooking oil, and cloth were rationed, and sales of rice were state-controlled (see Chapter 10).

Perhaps most important, the state also recognized private home ownership. Although there were no records or deeds to attest that the peasants owned their own homes, the lack of a document did not appear to bother Lo Chin-loung. She asserted that, "Everyone knows this house is ours"; and she added that when she and her husband built the extra rooms on their house, pre-empting the small area of land adjacent to their old house, no one contested this acquisition. They expected their two houses would be passed along in the family as long as survivors existed.

Should a dispute arise over ownership, the civil affairs department of the people's commune, assisted by a responsible member of the production brigade, would arbitrate. But in the case of an inheritance dispute, production brigade officials would discuss the quarrel with the survivors. The claimants would plead their cases; then, in the words of production brigade Chairman Ma Ping-kuan, the production brigade leaders would "help them reach a decision." If these methods did not achieve harmony, then the heirs could appeal to the higher authority

Middle-peasant Chen family home: living-dining area on left, kitchen shed on right.

of the civil affairs workers.

Ma cited several reasons for the Chinese peasants' apparent lack of concern for title deeds. For one thing, he said, the people still harbored some suspicions from the old days of Kuomintang and warlord rule, when individuals were often encumbered with voluminous but meaningless documents. A paper certificate had offered no guarantee against war, famine, or the debt-collectors, who could appropriate private property by foreclosing usurious loans. The people of Kwang Li said the existence of such documents today might be painfully reminiscent of the oppressive authority of past governments.

For the same reasons, the peasants of Kwang Li did not carry individual identity cards. Though such papers might seem innocuous, commune authorities told us that identification cards rekindled unwelcome memories of KMT police interrogations and conscription.

"The Kuomintang," recalled Ma Ping-kuan, "considered everyone without an I.D. card as a 'bad' person."

CCP authorities had learned from experience where their involvement in the private lives of the peasants should end and where further interference would arouse resentment. Besides, I.D.s were not really necessary in a place like Kwang Li, where everyone knew everyone else and strangers were easily spotted. However, each family maintained a registration book, and all the forms were filed in the production brigade offices.

9
SALARIES AND INCENTIVES

"Our rating is based on how hard we work," stated Hsieh Ping, the twenty-two-year-old round-faced farm laborer. "Those of us who are twenty to thirty years old and are stronger, naturally work harder."

"Of course," added Hsieh authoritatively, "attitude—if you are diligent or lazy—is always important."

Despite collectivization, individual effort was important and merited some rewards at Kwang Li People's Commune and throughout rural China in 1973. Generally speaking, each person performed one specific task every day. All jobs were scaled according to their difficulty and allotted a certain number of work-points, which ultimately determined the workers' salaries. Workers like Hsieh Ping were also rated according to their skill and dedication. So the total work-points she accumulated in a year reflected both the amount of labor she performed and its quality.

Aggregate work-points were vitally important because they determined the peasants' annual incomes.

Peasants like Hsieh Ping were paid twice a year. At midyear, they were paid a percentage of their production team's projected annual income and an allotment of food grain. In Kwang Li, the food grain was rice, the staple crop of Kwangtung Province; but in other areas of China it might be wheat or millet, for example, depending on the predominant cereal crop of that region. Hsieh Ping could also purchase some items, such as fish or chickens, on credit.

At the end of the year, each production team divided its harvest income minus taxes and other deductions by the combined total of the team-members' work-points to determine a money value for each work-point.

Based on each peasant's total work-points, the team accountants calculated individual salaries. The accountants then subtracted the salary advance and charges for the food grain issued at midyear, along with a charge for additional food grain issued at year's end; the remainder was paid in cash. Kwang Li's peasants earned an average income of (U.S.)$20 a month for agricultural work in 1973. But after deducting the average monthly allowance of fifty-three *catties* (fifty-eight pounds) of food grain (valued at roughly $2.50), a typical farm laborer earned a cash income of between $17 and $18 per month.

Work-points and production were coordinated through work groups of thirty to forty persons. By thoroughly organizing farm labor in work groups, the production teams endeavored to perform each day's tasks efficiently.

Since the peasants were generally allowed to choose their own work group, members tended to be close relatives and in-fighting was rare, according to the refugee from Kwang Li. He said there were often complaints and arguments, but he could not recall group members actually coming to blows.

On a typical sunny morning in the middle of the growing season, several hundred peasant farmers would converge in a large paddy. Lines of blue- and gray-clad figures, their faces shaded by saucer-shaped bamboo hats, meticulously combed through the rows of rice stalks, weeding, spreading fertilizer, and spraying insecticide. Like an intricate drill team, these collectivized work groups followed their master production plan, a cycle that was repeated in its entirety for every paddy through the development of two rice crops a year.

The agricultural workers at Kwang Li were ranked in three grades of proficiency. During most of the year, those persons falling into the same category earned the same amount for an average day's work in the fields. Usually, for example, a top-grade worker like Hsieh Ping would earn ten work-points a day; although one day she might be weeding and the next day spraying insecticide or performing another chore. Only during the so-called busy seasons did workers assigned the same proficiency rating begin to earn varying amounts of work-points, depending on how much extra labor they performed. These busy seasons were the March spring plowing season, the July harvest and transplanting season, the November harvest and transplanting time period, and December, when time was devoted to water conservation and other public works projects.

Those peasants who normally attained the highest evaluation merited an "A" rating. They were usually the young, able-bodied workers who performed the more difficult tasks. Slower workers received a middle, or "B" grade; and the elderly, "C" grade laborers usually performed easier chores, such as caring for a water buffalo or tending other farm animals.

In Sui Kang production brigade in 1973, the pay scale for a day's work performing average tasks in the fields was as follows:

RANK	GROWING SEASONS	BUSY SEASONS
"A", or highest grade	10.0 work-points	13.0 work-points
"B", or middle grade	9.5 work-points	12.5 work-points
"C", or lower grade	9.0 work-points	12.0 work-points

To a certain extent, the peasants decided among themselves which grades to assign to each other. Four times a year, the work groups of Sui Kang production brigade would meet in "self-education sessions." Sometimes they gathered at the side of a field, sometimes in the team neighborhood in the evening, to assign their grades. Afterwards, the work group leaders would get together with the production team leaders to reevaluate these assignments.

It was a painstaking process. The leaders would read aloud the name and work grade evaluation of each worker, and lengthy discussion would follow.

In our conversations with the field laborers, we learned that the peasants were graded not so much by their diligence as by their experience. Mature, seasoned laborers expected to be classified as grade "A" workers, whereas inexperienced peasants anticipated lower-grade designations. A twenty-eight-year-old field worker with a gold rim gleaming from her front tooth explained that she was promoted to the ranks of the grade "A" workers at the age of eighteen when she was married.

In practice, the variance in proficiency ratings did not create very large salary differentials, nor did we feel they carried as much weight as the work-point evaluations of individual jobs.

Seasonal variables and extra work opportunities were more important. The real chance to earn more work-points and hence a larger income lay not so much in the quality of the peasants' workmanship but in the amount of work they performed and the difficulty of the job they tackled.

In mass meetings convened at least twice a year, the members of Sui

Kang production brigade would debate their production team leaders' assessment of the value in work-points of each job. Weeding a paddy might be worth ten work-points a day; but pulling a cart filled with rocks would be assigned a value of fifteen work-points, since it was considerably more arduous.

"I'm sorry," apologized Liang Kung-ching, a twenty-one-year-old peasant hauling a cart piled high with sandstone boulders when we stopped to photograph him. He bowed his head, referring to his sweat-soaked, worn undershirt, tattered with holes like a sagging fishnet.

"I am doing heavy work," he explained, his hollow cheeks puffing with exhaustion, "so I did not dress well today."

Incentives have constantly stimulated debate, ever since the CCP took over in China. Radical elements have argued that China should follow the Marxist doctrine that proclaims, "From each according to his ability; to each according to his needs."

This ideal was more rigidly observed during the years of the Great Leap Forward economic plan from 1958 to 1962, when the people's communes were formed. In Kwang Li the people remembered that everyone was given "as much as they wanted to eat" during those years. The Marxist formula enabled the commune to accomplish its broad public works projects. But in the long run, as one peasant farmer summed up with agrarian logic, "It just didn't work." There was not enough food for everyone.

By 1973, necessity and experience altered the formula to, "From each according to his ability, to each according to his work."

An incentive system at Kwang Li was designed to insure that peasants would never ignore their allegiance to the group. Since the money value of each person's accumulated work-points was calculated as a fraction of the total annual income of each production team; no matter how many work-points a peasant might earn individually, if his production team as a whole did not work hard, his individual work-points would not be worth much. The bigger the whole pie, the bigger the size of each slice.

It was a subtle way of making every peasant's income depend upon how hard his neighbors worked. The system placed the weight of concerted peer pressure on any member of the production team who slackened in his or her efforts.

Liang Kung-ching hauls rocks.

These incentives were all the more important because the monetary value of a work-point varied widely, even between different production teams within the same production brigade or village. In 1972, the value of ten work-points, or an average day's work in Sui Kang production brigade ranged from 55 cents in some production teams to only 40 cents in others. The Kwang Li emigrant (refugee) later informed us in our Hong Kong interviews that in his production brigade, in 1973, this differential varied between 25 cents and 50 cents.

So, because of better teamwork, individuals in some production teams were earning considerably more than individuals in others.

Accounting for work-points was a daily ritual, apparently aimed at keeping the field workers on their toes. Every day, each production team's accountant, who was a cadre and often a CCP member, and his assistant would log the amount of work each peasant performed in a work-point ledger. Often they would personally tour the fields where groups were assigned.

Assessing individual achievements in a vast rice field was not as dizzying a chore as it might seem, for each peasant usually covered a defined area during a day's work. On a limited plot, the peasants concurred, it was fairly easy to determine if, for example, the weeding or insect-gathering had been successful.

When disputes arose, the farm workers said that the production team leader, the accountant, and the person whose work was in question might go to the fields for a reassessment. But the production team leader made the final decision.

Perhaps the most important form of incentive bonuses corresponded to the capitalistic concept of overtime. During the busy seasons, peasants accumulated more work-points for working longer hours or performing harder jobs (such as transplanting rice on an extensive area of land).

At the end of the year, field workers were also eligible for honors and rewards. Those peasants whose work-point totals placed them within the top 5 percent of their team would receive small gifts such as drinking cups. The names of the top 40 percent were also read aloud at an annual production team meeting.

There were negative incentives as well. Vice-Chairman Liang Weiming said that through "self criticism" the commune encouraged slackers to "overcome their mistakes."

*   *   *

During the Cultural Revolution (roughly 1966–1971), many people's communes were persuaded to institute what was known as the Tachai salary system, named after China's national model production brigade in Shansi Province. Under this system, each peasant received a certain number of work-points for a day's work. Peasants were judged not for how much work they performed, but for whether or not they were working up to their ability. So, for example, a "ten-point worker" would earn ten points, regardless of the assignment. Other aspects of the model Tachai system included rating the people's political consciousness and re-evaluating their grades every few days. In Hong Kong, the emigrant from Kwang Li recalled that under the Tachai system, the whole production team would meet to discuss evaluations, and later the team leadership committee would determine the final work-point allocations.

This young man described how the production team leaders conducted meetings through a procedure called "self-declaration and mass opinion." A peasant might declare he deserved a class "A" rating, but his colleagues might argue he only merited a "B" rank. The team leadership committee rendered the final judgment. The peasant could appeal his case to the team officials; but rarely would the leadership overturn their original ruling, the emigrant said.

The emigrant commented that, in general, Tachai-type evaluation was "not too unfair," since judgments were based on a majority vote among the production team committee members.

In 1971, Peking backed down from its more radical Cultural Revolution position and announced that those people's communes that were sufficiently "advanced" in political consciousness could revert to their former practices of work-point evaluation.

So, early in 1972, after a decision which the refugee recalled "came from above," Kwang Li returned to the old incentive system. A formal announcement stated that the commune was "initiating" on an "experimental" basis a system of salary payment. Now they would give greater priority to the difficulty of tasks, rather than to individual ratings.

With an amused smile, the young emigrant noted that village officials had insisted this was a new system having no relationship with the past. Nevertheless, the peasants recognized it as similar, if not identical, to the old payment method. They identified the old method with former head of state Liu Shao-chi, who was severely denounced throughout China during the Cultural Revolution.

The emigrant added that although the incentive system adopted in early 1972 was still in effect when he left Kwang Li over two years later, commune bureaucrats were still declaring the system was provisional. He surmised this was the officials' way of coping with the possibility of another challenge to the incentive system in the future.

The peasants welcomed the revival of the piece-work payment plan, the emigrant said. As a result, they were accomplishing their tasks in less time than they had under the Tachai plan. But this did not mean the commune's productivity had improved. Instead, knowing they would receive their work-points when they completed a task, the peasants worked more assiduously. For example, they finished in six days' time what they would have performed in ten days under the Tachai directive. Then, he said, the people spent the extra four days pursuing private side-line occupations, such as collecting firewood, for their personal benefit.

Subsequently, added the young man in Hong Kong, the peasants were more content, and things had settled down, with fewer arguments in the work groups than before 1972.

Although the Cultural Revolution was aimed at motivating the Chinese people to follow what Peking called the "socialist road," at Kwang Li and elsewhere, Chinese leaders found it necessary to integrate some suspiciously capitalistic incentives and rewards into their socialist system. It was debatable whether these concessions signified a failure of what Chairman Mao called the "Great Proletarian Cultural Revolution," but their application indicated that the Chinese leadership was able to recognize and adapt to the weaknesses and strengths of human nature.

10
AGRICULTURE

"We must concentrate on agriculture," affirmed the vice-chairman of Kwang Li's Revolutionary Committee with a joyous grin.

Then, as though he were reciting biblical commandments, still beaming broadly and spreading his arms for emphasis, Liang Wei-ming launched into a hortatory statement that rolled automatically from his lips.

"As Chairman Mao has said, 'Take agriculture as the main foundation and industry as the main direction.' " (Industry can only develop with agriculture.)

Finally came Liang's summation, which the CCP had etched deeply in the consciousness of every peasant in China: "Food grain is the key link!"

In conformity with CCP exhortations to diversify crops to create more self-sufficient communities and to improve the diet of the peasants, who formerly subsisted mainly on rice, the people of Kwang Li had transformed a one-crop (rice) economy into a more diversified agricultural output.

To demonstrate this accomplishment, visitors to Kwang Li were greeted with saucers filled with candied fruits—water chestnuts, lotus root, and yams—all of which were grown on the commune and processed and preserved by the local confectionery factory.

Each production brigade and production team attempted to diversify its output to augment its livelihood. The collective farmers supplemented rice cultivation with so-called "industrial crops" such as sugar cane and peanuts, and with orchards, tangerine gardens, livestock breeding, animal husbandry, and various vegetable crops. Diversification carried over into the private sector, too. Families were encouraged to raise pigs; the commune leaders hoped to increase Kwang Li's porcine population to fifty thousand—more pigs than people!—by the end of 1973.

Despite diversification, most of the commune's ten thousand arable acres, spreading from the mossy mountains to the muddy West River, were devoted to rice cultivation. As Liang Wei-ming constantly reminded us, food grain was truly the key link to the peasants' survival.

The commune harvested two rice crops, one which grew from March fifteenth to the end of June, another from the end of July to late October. Commune farmers were even attempting to cultivate three crops, but as of 1973 this effort had not gone beyond experimentation.

Kwang Li's peasants cultivated three varieties of rice. Scanning the paddy fields in the middle of the growing season, one could see early-ripening rice about to yield, middle-ripening rice sprouting leaves, and tender sprigs of late-ripening rice just thrusting above the irrigated plain.

During May, when the fertile farmlands were yielding up their bounty, the work groups were busily engaged in a variety of tasks: spraying insecticide, weeding, and undertaking "field management," such as digging ditches to drain water from potentially waterlogged fields.

The production brigades bought insecticide from the county government. Ten cents' worth sufficed to spray one *mou* (one-sixth of an acre) of land.

The commune had been steadily raising its rice production starting from only about 4.7 million pounds reportedly grown before 1949 to 50 million pounds in 1972. In 1964, according to Liang, Kwang Li surpassed a national target by harvesting 5,280 pounds of rice per acre of cultivated paddy; and in 1972, this figure had climbed to nearly 7,920 pounds per acre.

Rice was only part of the Kwang Li success story as reported by Liang Wei-ming. About 60 percent of the commune's land, he eulogized, was devoted to the cultivation of one or more second crops. Not only were the peasants at Kwang Li intercropping other foods amid the rice (in the same field, shoots of sugar cane were pushing up next to the rice seedlings), but also the peasants were accelerating rice production and implementing long-range plans to reclaim the rugged mountain lands for farming. And, just as the peasants cultivated rice in semiannual phases, the commune grew two annual crops of peanuts and sugar cane. Research also involved crops other than rice. For example, the

Weeding the communal paddy field during the growing season.

commune was trying to grow winter wheat, which was not native to Kwangtung Province's subtropical climate.

Kwang Li's reported achievements in rice production were echoed by data for each of the major foods the commune grew. By the end of 1973, Liang Wei-ming expected the commune as a whole to increase its total agricultural output by as much as 10 or 12 percent over the previous year.

Without consulting his account books, Liang proudly enumerated a long list of statistics, tallying the harvests of various crops. His enthusiasm for these numbers and the progress they represented endowed the cold figures with vitality and warmth. His words evoked a stirring, cinematic sequence of images: peasants threshing grain, their mud-caked hands rhythmically pulling ripe vegetables from the ground.

Liang's statistics dramatized a saga of rural achievement. The peasants were steadily increasing their cultivation of sugar cane, peanuts (which could be processed on the commune and used for cooking oil), hemp, tangerines, lychees, longans, pears, bananas, water chestnuts, lotus roots, garlic, and many other crops. Kwang Li's workers also toppled timber and collected resin and honey (see Appendix, Agricultural Statistics).

Not all the produce raised at Kwang Li was consumed locally. The commune sold many products to the cities to pay for operations and purchases.

Distribution of rice followed an established system. First, the commune decided how much rice it needed to distribute locally as part of the peasants' salaries and for rationed sale in Kwang Li town. Town-dwellers received graded allotments: fifty pounds a month for "heavy workers," forty pounds for "ordinary workers," thirty-three pounds for clerks, and various-sized portions for children according to age. At prices established in 1957 (see Appendix), commune members could purchase rice in three categories, according to quality. The commune also kept aside some food grain to feed its animals and as seed, and stored a large amount as reserves.

The remainder of the commune rice harvest went to the state, to feed China's urban population and fill the national grain reserves. So important was rice to the Chinese economy that the commune paid its taxes to the government in the form of rice and sold its surplus rice to the state as well. Liang Wei-ming claimed that the state did not dictate how much rice the commune must contribute. The commune, he insisted, made this decision. Of the 50 million pounds harvested in its 1972 rice crops, Kwang Li was able to provide 23 million pounds, or nearly half the total crop, for the central government. Most of that, some 20.5 million pounds, was in the form of outright sales, but a small portion went to fill the tax requirement.

Despite China's authoritarian system, the state did not appear to exact a significant amount of rice in actual taxes. Surprisingly, the agricultural tax in rice had remained the same ever since it was established in 1953, when the tax was assigned at 9 percent of that year's total production. That amount—2,530,000 pounds—remained the tax assessment in 1973, even though the total output had just about doubled since then. So the commune now paid a tax to the state amounting to only about 5 percent of its harvests. In the future, as commune production rose yearly, the commune expected to pay proportionately less and less to the state in taxes.

In addition to the rice that was consumed or sold to the state, the commune encouraged peasants to store six months' supply of rice in their homes, in case of war or natural calamity.

In 1972, Kwang Li's private families stored a total of 1,760,000 pounds of reserve rice in their homes. The production brigades kept another 250,000 pounds, the production teams stored 1,275,000 pounds, and the commune administration maintained its own supply of 22,000 pounds. Production brigades kept their collective rice reserves in village granaries such as the converted temple in Sui Kang village.

Like most peasant households, Lo Chin-loung's family of four adults kept over 750 pounds of unhusked rice in their home. The family raised cats to prevent mice from invading these precious stores, and they said that by keeping the rice dry in a tall woven bamboo bin, they prevented damage from insects.

In 1972, foreign observers believe China's national grain output fell sharply because of a nationwide drought. In that year, Kwang Li, which was located in the monsoon belt, increased its rice harvest. Nevertheless, commune officials claimed the state did not requisition additional food grain from this prosperous area to feed the drought-stricken parts of the country.

"In every people's commune and production brigade in China," said Liang Wei-ming, "people are doing the same thing: storing rice in case of a shortage." So, he reported, when shortages developed, the inhabitants of the drought-stricken areas consumed their own local reserves. Since Kwang Li increased its production in 1972, he added, the commune sold 400,000 more pounds to the state that year than previously. But he claimed this was a voluntary sale, not a government requisition.

The commune constantly rotated its domestic rice reserves, consuming the stored rice and replacing the reserves with each new harvest.

In a two-story brick granary in Kwang Li town, the rice was secured from the natural elements and from human threats. The commune used rat poison to protect its valuable stocks from vermin. About once a week in summer, teams of inspectors visited the granary to plunge yard-long metal thermometers into the ten-foot-deep piles of unhusked rice. If the rice was overheating, they opened the doors and windows and spread out the rice, to reduce its vulnerability to insects, which increased at higher temperatures.

Commune militia members guarded the granary from another supposed danger: sabotage from class enemies. Whether class enemies or even criminals really threatened the granary did not appear to make much difference. In the countryside, there was a cultivated fear of anti-CCP elements who, the granary director said he believed, supposedly wanted "to destroy our socialist system." This notion was the rationale for posting armed guards at the granary every night. However, the young militiaman from the middle-peasant Chen family, who faithfully stood watch by a granary night after night, said he could not personally recall when any of these installations had been attacked or even threatened.

After communization, Kwang Li's farmers were exhorted to start raising livestock and to undertake animal husbandry, which previously they had not been able to afford to undertake on a large scale. So, besides the fifty thousand privately and commune-owned pigs, in 1973 Kwang Li supported thirty-seven hundred water buffaloes, thirteen hundred cows, and more chickens than anyone could count, pecking along the dirt paths of the villages.

Given the rural emphasis on increasing production, and taking into account the improved security the commune system provided, it was probably not surprising that the only inhabitants of the commune who carried life insurance were not people, but pigs. The residents of the family pigsty were covered by an unusual actuarial system: *after* the peasants sold their *healthy* animals to the state, they paid a premium of about $1.10, to be deposited in a special account at a commune veterinary station. If a pig died, the veterinarian would compensate the pig's owner from this communal fund. Compensation was not equal to what the farmers could earn from a sale, but it covered the cost of growing the animals. Grown pigs, weighing about forty pounds, brought about $45 or more when they were sold to the commune's purchasing office. Insurance compensation was only 10 cents a pound for pigs weighing under about five pounds and 29 cents a pound for those exceeding that weight.

This insurance system, which was introduced in 1958, encouraged peasants to take the risk of raising pigs and to take good care of their animals. It seemed to work, since just about every house in Sui Kang village had a full pigsty, and the village echoed with the metallic thud of chopping knives preparing fodder.

Pig insurance fees also covered the costs of inoculating the animals against disease, a procedure repeated every three months. No insurance policies protected cows and buffaloes, but their inoculations only cost about 60 cents a year. Commune officials claimed that these efforts had virtually wiped out serious animal disease.

Kwang Li employed thirty-two veterinarians, trained at specialized schools or educated on the job. Some, like thirty-two-year-old Lung Hou-pin, who served in Kwang Li's veterinary station since 1958, learned about raising animals from childhood.

"My father is a farmer," said this slim, earnest man, "so I like this occupation. I think livestock and poultry are lovely." (Yes, "lovely"! The interpreter repeated the word, to be sure Lung meant to say it that way.) Lung, who had seven years of education in his village, attended a short-term veterinary training school in the county seat at the commune's expense. His salary was $18.50 a month, part of that paid in food grain.

At least one veterinarian was assigned to each agricultural production brigade, and six specialists, including Lung Hou-pin, devoted their full-time efforts to manning the commune livestock veterinary station.

Veterinary station workers supervised breeding and disease prevention as well as animal care. In a laboratory that boasted one of the few refrigerators on the commune, the veterinarians performed blood tests and administered vaccines and treatment. They also conducted research. The veterinary station kept over 110 pigs and several dozen chickens for experiments in breeding and feeding. For instance, the specialists had raised some pigs on various types of fodder, trying cooked and uncooked diets and assessing the results. In one recent experiment, the commune veterinarians trained pigs to eat water hyacinths, a nuisance plant that formerly had clogged the waterways.

Mechanization of agriculture was one CCP goal that stoked the flames of Vice-Chairman Liang Wei-ming's ardor even more than usual.

In 1973, the commune owned only seventy-one tractors for its ten thousand acres of cultivated land; and the vast proportion of the work was still hand labor. Kwang Li had the funds to purchase more tractors, but Vice-Chairman Liang said that the government could not manufacture enough to fulfill China's requirements. Each year the commune submitted an order for vehicles that was reduced by someone higher up the chain of command. In 1972 the commune petitioned for fifty-three tractors but was allotted only twenty-nine; in 1973 Kwang Li's allotment of thirty-seven tractors fell far short of their request for seventy-six.

Because motor vehicles were in such short supply, the commune used its sixteen large tractors and fifty-five "walking" tractors for purposes other than field work. Tractors were employed as trucks to transport goods, and for grading mountain terrain. (Just about every possible parcel of land at Kwang Li was cultivated; even in the craggy mountains, the peasants had carved terraces to extract crops from the soil.) Most of the vehicles on the commune roads were Kwang Li's four thousand three hundred registered bicycles, whose owners paid an annual tax of $1.20.

It would be a long time before China's farmers could rely fully upon mechanical aid for farming or transportation. Water buffalo and humans were still the prevailing means of carrying goods; and lines of men and women, laden under the shoulder yokes that Chinese peasants have borne for centuries, were commonly encountered trudging along the dusty commune roads.

Tractors, which cost $4,800 for the large model and $1,500 for the "walking" model, belonged to the commune, the production brigades, or the production teams. The production brigades maintained most of their own equipment and even handled small repairs, but the commune's agricultural machinery maintenance and repair shop tackled major repairs.

The tractor repair station, with its fifty-five employees, had been in operation since May 1966. The workers could repair four or five tractors a week, as well as fixing threshing machines. Whoever owned each machine would pay for the repair job.

Vertical columns of bold Chinese characters framed a doorway of the machine shop. "Self-reliance; hard struggle," they declared. "Prepare for war, calamity. Everything for the people."

When he had learned that his production team planned to purchase tractors, twenty-two-year-old Chen Siu-yang (of the poor-peasant Chens) said he had requested to learn how to drive and repair a tractor.

"At that time," said Chen, squinting a smile, "I knew mechanization was the basic way out for China, and I thought in this way, I could help to develop agriculture."

About one month later, when his production team received its first tractor, Chen was chosen as one of the team members who were trained and later took turns driving, maintaining, and repairing the vehicle. Perhaps he was selected, Chen speculated, "because the team knew I was interested in machinery."

Ostensibly motivated by idealism, Chen might also have been thinking of his own welfare. In 1972, when he began working on the tractor force, his yearly salary increased by about $15 and he received eleven more pounds of food grain a month. It was impossible for an outsider to estimate whether personal gain influenced this young peasant's ambition. But he was joining in the drive to build the future mechanized China with genuine enthusiasm.

11
INDUSTRY

"My future is closely linked with the future of my country," chirped nineteen-year-old Lee Chieh-ping crisply, with a casual bounce of her pigtails. Lee assembled electric motors in the small factory and repair shop located in a grassy hollow below the river embankment just outside Kwang Li town.

"Of course," continued this straightforward, moon-faced woman, "I want to be a better worker."

Her coworker, thirty-one-year-old Hsien Chi-chuan, depicted his ambition as a purely institutional matter. Said Hsien, with an oblique glance, "As an ordinary worker, my desire is to produce more goods."

Kwang Li's factory workers repaired farm machinery; manufactured electric motors for rice-threshers; and produced a variety of other farm machines, planers, and pliers. According to factory officials, some of the heavy machinery used in the small plant was fabricated on the commune.

Nearly half the work performed at the factory directly benefited Kwang Li's indigenous population, demonstrating once again how this commune and others like it were seeking self-sufficiency and attempting to diversify the economy. By rapidly building up small, local industries like this one, along with large plants in urban areas, Peking was fulfilling a Mao dictum: "walking on two legs"—developing China's economy slowly and realistically, utilizing local resources to the fullest, while simultaneously making long-term investments in heavy industry.

Other, smaller industries also contributed to Kwang Li's well-rounded development. No less than seventeen brick kilns fired their products from local materials; an aromatic winery converted fermented rice, cassava, and wheat into wine; and other local enterprises manufactured wooden farm tools, sickles, and starch.

Factory worker Hsien Chi-chuan sublimated personal ambition in favor of production.

By far the largest and most impressive industry at Kwang Li was its agricultural machinery repair and manufacturing plant, where Lee Chieh-ping and Hsien Chi-chuan worked.

The main factory room and its annexes were built directly on the bare earth. High ceilings provided ventilation in the sticky summer weather. Lee, Hsien, and their colleagues worked their machines eight hours a day, seated on either side of broad aisles. Electric light bulbs suspended above the workers supplemented sunlight that poured in from open windows.

As in most public buildings at Kwang Li, the factory's plain brick walls were plastered with colorful posters. The pictures portrayed workers, forging metal and leading parades of what appeared to be a sturdy, mixed-race proletariat. At one end of the largest room, an oversized photograph of Chairman Mao, who had encouraged rural areas like this one to industrialize, dominated the work area.

Kwang Li's factory had not attained total self-reliance, however. This factory had expanded quickly, growing from a simple blacksmithing shop in the early 1950s to a plant with nearly one hundred employees. But this was possible only with outside help. The plant managers had to hire 15 percent of their workers from outside the commune, since not enough skilled workers were available locally.

The commune was not above bending the principle of self-reliance, in the pursuit of a goal as worthy as increased production.

The factory's most rapid expansion came in 1972. To meet growing local pressure for more mechanical repairs, and to manufacture pliers to sell to other parts of China, three new workshops were constructed adjacent to the original one-room shop; and eighteen more workers were recruited, to create a staff of ninety-six. The commune doubled the number of machines producing pliers from four to eight, and the factory acquired eight additional lathes.

As a result, in 1973 officials estimated yearly income at the factory would reach $180,000 a year.

Kwang Li's factory workers seemed too dedicated to be believed. Did they really sublimate all their personal goals in favor of the good of the community?

A closer examination revealed that industrial workers like Lee Chieh-ping and Hsien Chi-chuan actually had much to gain personally by pledging their commitment to the common fortune. These factory workers' slice of well-being depended on the overall success of their

The main assembly room of the factory and repair shop.

factory's financial pie, much as the welfare of Kwang Li's peasant farmers depended upon their production team's collective harvest. Factory workers' salaries were determined by a system similar to the incentive program that spurred on the agricultural sector.

Machine shop workers were categorized into four salary levels, similar to the farmers' proficiency ratings. At the bottom were the apprentices, who earned about $16 a month in 1973.

A second-level worker who had been employed at this factory since she left school at age sixteen, Lee Chieh-ping took home $18.50 a month, about the same amount as a field laborer.

Factory workers expected promotions in the same way the peasant field-hands expected to receive certain proficiency ratings. Promotions were supposed to be based on periodic evaluations, but there was an unofficial but fairly rigid advancement schedule linked to the number of years a worker had been employed at the factory.

Every three months, in meetings similar to the peasant farmers' evaluations, the factory workers would meet in small groups to appraise each other's performance. At the end of the year, they were supposed to decide who would graduate to the next level. Apparently workers were not usually promoted until they spent a generally agreed-upon time at each level.

The workers said that promotion to the second salary level came automatically after the first year of employment. And, after a certain time on the job, Lee Chieh-ping could look forward to her next salary bracket, that of a third-level worker, at about $22 a month.

When he had graduated from primary school at the age of sixteen, Hsien Chi-chuan, then a peasant farmer, told his production brigade leader that he would like to contribute to the commune's industrial development, which was then in its infancy. He had demonstrated a mechanical aptitude working with the brigade's farm machinery. So, when the commune labor bureau recruited factory workers, he was chosen for this privileged position.

Now, with fifteen years' experience in the factory, Hsien Chi-chuan had risen to the ranks of the fourth salary level. He earned the highest-level salary paid at the factory, about $25 per month.

One member of the factory's managing Revolutionary Committee noted that there was not much differentiation between the work levels. But the committee chairman said he expected that in time, as the work at the factory became more complex and as the workers developed more expertise, new grades would be created. Some day, workers like Lee and Hsien would aspire to as many as eight grades of achievement, assuming the factory grew and its products developed.

It was easy to predict who would move ahead. Each month, every worker was assigned a production target. On the wall of the main building, where the drills and lathes whirred, hung a blackboard. White painted lines divided the board into columns. Each column represented one worker's achievement. Chalk check marks indicated the worker's assigned goal, and movable red arrows were adjusted daily as each worker met or surpassed that day's goal. The procedure seemed ominous, but Hsien Chi-chuan noted that in the past year, every employee was able to meet or exceed his or her individual quota with no apparent distress.

Since the salary scale increased only when the plant's overall income rose, there was plenty of incentive to meet or exceed production targets.

Besides individual promotion and the prestige of an advancing red arrow, there was also a chance for material rewards. Every three months, workers were eligible for certificates of honor. At the annual appraisal meeting, those employees who surpassed their targets would receive small gifts, usually teacups. These gifts could not exceed $3.50 in value, and no cash awards were permitted. In 1972, because he topped his quota by 12 percent, Hsien Chi-chuan, the senior grade worker, received a bonus: a vacuum flask.

In addition, workers like Hsien, who lived at the factory dormitory six days a week, also received free lodging and meals—a considerable premium in an economy where food was the major expense.

At Kwang Li, these factory workers were among the most exalted members of the commune society. They earned the best salaries, far in excess of peasant farmers' earnings, and they were entitled to health and insurance benefits that were more substantial than those available to the peasant field workers.

About three times a week, the factory workers assembled in political study groups of about ten persons each. The discussions were organized by a group leader who was usually a member of the plant's Revolutionary Committee.

Lee Chieh-ping and her female coworkers also attended staff women's meetings once a week. Discussions focused on such subjects as "How to learn from heroes and heroines." Lee said the women in the

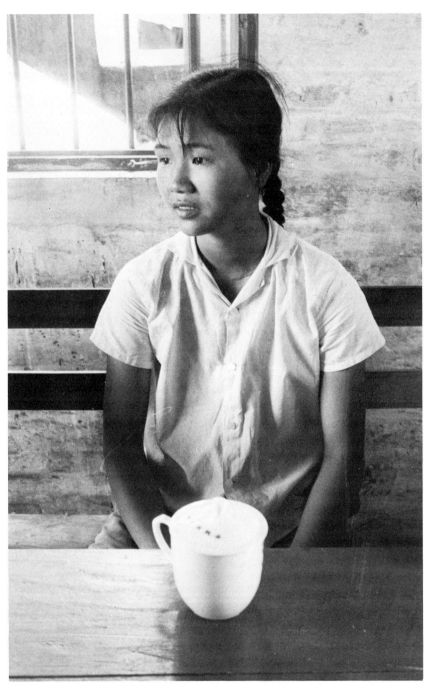

Lee Chieh-ping assembled electric motors in the small commune factory.

factory exhibited little interest in women's rights, for, she claimed, both sexes in this factory were equal, and "women are promoted just as quickly as men."

There were differences in the lifestyles of male and female employees, though. In contrast to Hsien Chi-chuan, who was provided with a bunk in the factory dormitory and enjoyed meals in the canteen because he lived too far from the factory to commute, Lee Chieh-ping lived with her parents in Kwang Li town and paid for her own food. Generally, men came to the factory from all over the commune and beyond its borders; but women were only recruited from the nearby town, where they returned for lunch and in the evenings.

Lee's father worked in a rice mill, and her mother worked in a restaurant in town. Unlike most Chinese families, Lee said her parents did not ask her to give them part of her pay check. Since her expenses amounted to only about $10 a month, including the $6 she spent on food, she had bought her own bicycle and was able to put aside $200 in a savings account. She was saving "for no special purpose," she told us.

Hsien Chi-chuan, who had a wife and two children and owned a home in his native village, had only managed to accumulate $150 in his savings account, but his family owned a sewing machine as well as a bicycle.

Hsien spent his one day off a week with his family. Lee, who was single, said she visited the nearest city, Chao Ch'ing (Shiu Hing), fifteen miles away, to see a movie; or she read technical magazines, newspapers, and literary magazines in her spare time.

Commune youth did not have much opportunity for travel, and they did not cite traveling among their personal ambitions. But when asked if she would like to visit other places, Lee Chieh-ping said dreamily she would like to go to Canton, "because it's nearest," and maybe, some day, Peking.

12
LIFESTYLE AND LEISURE

One evening, residents of Kwang Li town and nearby hamlets packed into the commune's small amphitheater for a "big match." Kwang Li's men's and women's basketball teams were challenging teams from another commune. Several thousand spectators filled the stone-seated gallery, and hundreds of others stood in the dusty darkness at the far walkways, craning their necks to see the brightly lighted court.

Despite their interest, the crowd was restrained. The athletes received polite applause when they marched into the arena, and throughout the evening, the spectators never cheered or booed. Their enthusiasm was so egalitarian they applauded vigorously whenever each team scored.

At intermission, just as in half-time in an American stadium, the teams fell into formation to spell a message on the court. The Chinese characters spelled out, "Learn from each other." In this spirit, Kwang Li's women's team went on to victory, 42 to 38, over the team from the commune across the river. After the final whistle, the teams abruptly formed parallel lines, marched towards each other, and shook hands in a ritual that could only have been designed to emphasize good sportsmanship.

Many foreigners shared a common preconception that Chinese peasants rose before dawn and toiled in the fields from daybreak until sunset, 365 days a year. But another myth about the CCP regimen dissolved into reality when we observed that during the slack season, while the rice was growing, the field workers often did not go to work until 8:00 A.M. They worked at an easy pace, took a two-hour lunch break, and returned home by 5:00.

In fact, unless they performed specialized tasks far from their production team's fields, such as tending the production brigade's tangerines or, like Chen Chi-fun, surveying for a new brigade power station, the peasants could usually manage to go home for lunch. Only during planting and harvest time would workers often eat at paddy-side.

The intensity of labor accelerated sharply during these busy seasons. That's when the peasants worked longer hours and earned extra work-points. But in the growing seasons, the field workers settled down to a less hectic routine.

Work at Kwang Li had evolved considerably from the bitter toil of Chinese peasants through the centuries. Although they labored diligently and often arduously, the farmers and factory workers were assured plenty of free time and many alternatives as to how to spend it.

Just about every evening, there were organized events in all but the most remote villages on the commune. This schedule probably dampened peasant longing for the attractions of big-city life and helped keep them contented "down on the farm."

Many production brigades showed films, and a motion picture projection team traveled on foot to the mountain areas. Admission was inexpensive: The peasants only paid 2½ cents for seats at film versions of revolutionary operas and dramas such as *The Red Detachment of Women.*

"We have movies every week," said Liang Wei-ming, "mostly Chinese, but also Rumanian, Albanian, Korean, and Vietnamese." Foreign films were especially welcomed after the initial phases of the Cultural Revolution, when the number of state-approved Chinese films shrank to a mere handful. Commune citizens like factory worker Lee Chieh-ping could also travel to cinemas in the nearest city.

Previously, local culture in the indigent areas of China was limited to religious festivities and traveling operas and puppet troupes. Community participation in the arts was practically nonexistent. Culture for the most part thrived in the cities, so the absentee landlords lived and spent their leisure time there.

Now the CCP encouraged the peasants' artistic creativity, under the limits of the CCP dictum that art must serve the state and the people.

Kwang Li People's Commune supported its own propaganda team, which entertained the members of each production brigade monthly with medleys of songs and dances. Some of the skits and songs they composed were surprisingly sophisticated and lively. The shows were replete with colorful scenery, lighting effects, and costumes, including the only post-kindergarten *skirts* on the commune.

Village schools produced their own stage performances. Their efforts bore witness to the fact that not everything in China was accomplished with drill-team efficiency. We watched one group of about a dozen pink-cheeked teen-aged girls rehearsing in a shady space behind their primary school for a forthcoming holiday performance. As their teacher vainly counted out a regular rhythm, the children made one false start after another, chanting an off-key encomium to Chairman Mao Tse-tung.

Commune members were encouraged to submit poems and articles based on their own experiences to local and state magazines. The commune organized its own "journalistic" team, which reported on commune activities for national news organs such as the *People's Daily.*

Once a week, the commune staged athletic contests between local teams. The most popular sports were volleyball, table tennis, and basketball—low-budget athletics that were available all over the commune. Schools organized intramural athletic competitions, and children gathered informally after class for volleyball and basketball in the schoolyards.

The commune loudspeakers also belched martial music three times a day for organized calisthenics in all schools and offices.

Political study meetings and organizations such as women's groups, the Young Communists League, and various professional associations convened in the hours after work was finished. These meetings hardly constituted voluntary recreation, but they proved that life for the Chinese peasants was no longer the twenty-four-hours-a-day ceaseless toil it once was.

There was also plenty of spontaneous amusement. The peasants would get together in the evenings to chat or play cards, and the night air would ring with caustic Cantonese humor.

Wider communication was another radical change that accompanied the new way of life for Kwang Li's peasants.

Social intercourse was extremely limited in the Chinese countryside before 1949. Within the hundred-square-mile area of the people's commune at Kwang Li, people spoke several often mutually unintelligible dialects. The farmers of the lowland plain spoke what ostensibly was Cantonese; but our interpreter, who was educated in Canton, had difficulty understanding some of them. Among the hills, just a stone's throw away, another ethnic group, the Hakkas, conversed in a dialect that was entirely their own. Isolated for centuries by prejudice and poor transportation, the Hakkas had preserved their unique speech patterns.

Previously, Chinese from different areas often could only communicate in writing. Now a CCP decision to institute Mandarin Chinese *(p'u t'ung hua)* as the common dialect was eliminating language barriers in Kwang Li and throughout China. Schools in China were universally teaching Mandarin, so that eventually the people of one commune could converse with each other, as well as with natives of Shanghai, Szechwan, or far-off Peking. The administrative benefits of this decree were obvious.

P'u t'ung hua was not yet the universal tongue at Kwang Li. The older peasants and smaller children spoke only their native dialect, Cantonese. But those peasants aged from about ten to thirty-five could speak Mandarin, and this represented a major breakthrough.

Formerly, because they could not communicate with people from another part of their own market district, much less from the far reaches of Kwangtung Province, the people of this area were functionally isolated. Since few peasants could read, even when printed materials were available in pre-1949 society, these people had only a sketchy perception, if any, of China, and an even vaguer conception of the rest of the world. The introduction of a national dialect shattered those linguistic barriers. Today, ironically, even though they had newspapers, a broadcasting station, films, propaganda shows, and educators describing the "world situation," to most of the older peasants at Kwang Li, the "outside world" still began just beyond the borders of their villages. Of faraway places like Canton, Shanghai, and Peking, they had only vague notions; and they had only the most puerile concept of foreign nations. The younger peasants had a much better appreciation of the vast totality of China, but their awareness of the world beyond China's borders was constrained by the government, which controlled the media.

At Kwang Li, the peasants enjoyed more exposure to outsiders than on most other people's communes, for their model commune was visited occasionally by foreigners from Canton. Nevertheless, many villagers counted us as the first non-Chinese they had ever seen.

When Paul Steinle first visited Kwang Li in 1972, he asked to tour a people's commune where no journalists had previously traveled. At that time, the outhouse signs near commune headquarters were labeled in Chinese only, so he had to ask which door was for men. By the time he returned, six months later, more foreigners had apparently visited Kwang Li, for on the doors were neatly lettered the words *Men* and *Women.*

Foreigner in colloquial Cantonese is *fan kuai lo,* "white foreign devil," since Caucasians originally reminded the Chinese of pale ghosts or devils. When we asked one wily commune dweller if he had ever seen a *fan kuai lo,* he replied, "Oh, yes—but he was a *black* 'foreign-devil'!"

Lo Chin-loung once visited Canton, a three-hour bus trip from Kwang Li. But it was not until 1972 that she saw foreigners for the first time, taking photographs in her village. She knew that relations with the United States had improved, but she could not recall hearing of the U.S. liaison office in Peking. When asked to identify China's enemies, she referred sweepingly to "Chiang Kai-shek and the Imperialists."

For youth on the commune, the geography of China was a familiar concept. Many of them had traveled to other parts of their province, and uniformly they expressed a desire to see more of their homeland. Yet even these earnest young peasants had only a faint inkling of the customs and cultures of other countries. On our visit, we distributed scenic postcards of the United States as token gifts. When we showed some young people a postcard photograph of a skyscraper (Boston's Prudential Tower), they asked, "Is that your house?"

We were assured there were no restrictions on travel for those who could afford it and that people could travel within Kwangtung Province without special documents. However, outside the province, commune authorities said letters of identification were required "for convenience." At the end of our visit, a commune clerk rode with us to Canton to spend the weekend with her sister, who lived there.

Bus travel was popular, and five buses a day connected Kwang Li with the cities and towns of the province.

Travel within China was a possibility, but leaving the commune and getting a job elsewhere was extremely rare. Job mobility was practically unknown in Chinese society. As production brigade leader Ma Ping-kuan noted, "It is hard to find a job elsewhere without an introduction."

Since Kwang Li was less than one day's trip from Canton, it had been common before 1949 for young men to leave the countryside to seek a higher standard of living in the city. Middle-aged males who had made that pilgrimage testified that it usually led to disappointment. But this alternative no longer existed. Employment was tightly controlled by the bureaucracy, so few young men and women of Kwang Li could harbor any expectations of leaving the commune.

The only peasants to leave the commune officially in recent years were seven or eight members of Ma's brigade who were transferred to other people's communes in 1972 by a county labor bureau decision. Peasant youngsters could not pick up stakes and seek their fortune, as Ma Ping-kuan did in his youth and the young Mao Tse-tung did in his day.

The nearest border was Hong Kong, but it was taboo. Suggesting that the young peasants might visit there elicited blank looks or hasty protestations of, "Oh, not for me!"

But in China's cities, they did talk about Hong Kong. In fact, said the emigrant from Kwang Li, who was in his early twenties, young people in Canton would get together just to talk about Hong Kong and how to get there. He said such discussions were particularly common among students like himself whom the CCP had "sent down" to the communes for an indefinite time. So accurate were the descriptions, the young man said, that when he finally arrived in Hong Kong, nothing about the modern, congested city surprised him.

"I knew exactly what to expect," he remarked glibly.

From ancient until modern times, the major historical, cultural, and philosophical trends that molded the fate of China had left only minor impressions in Kwang Li. Dynasties came and fell, but what really affected the people there were the whims of the local landlords and the vicissitudes of the elements.

So, too, organized religion passed these people by. In this particular region, the closest thing to religion was an animistic ancestor-worship. There were no monasteries or centers of Buddhist learning in the rugged mountains of Kwang Li or among its impoverished paddy fields. There was no record of Christian missionaries either. Religion meant ritual: lighting joss sticks (incense) before portraits of ancestors and ancestral tablets or Buddhist deities, sacrificing offerings of food, donating money and gifts to the temple, and sweeping the ancestors' graves during the Ching Ming festival.

When the Communists came to Kwang Li, they decreed that reason should replace religion and science should supplant superstition. They substituted the portrait of Chairman Mao for the ancestor pictures and tablets.

Communism became the new religion. Not only did it represent an entire way of life, but also it entailed a set of rituals and doctrine.

The peasants of Kwang Li sacrificed no rigid set of beliefs when they accepted the CCP canons. All they had abandoned was a religion of empty ritual and a faith without hope, the CCP declared.

"Praying to Buddha never helped us before," said Liang Wei-ming, "so it was not difficult to convince people to stop practicing religion."

We could not assess the validity of Liang's statement or evaluate the sincerity of the people's feeling. But we could confirm that the CCP had virtually eradicated the old religion and replaced it with the new cult of Chairman Mao. Material traces of the old practices had vanished completely at Kwang Li, because the great flood of 1949 had destroyed most of the ancestral temples on the river plain.

The people of this rational new China gave up what Liang called "feudalistic practices"—burning incense, kneeling, and praying. And the emigrant in Hong Kong said that the authorities treated particularly harshly anyone who was discovered surreptitiously selling religious articles such as incense.

Commune authorities removed the ancestral graves that occupied fertile farmland and transferred their contents to the mountains. They now recommended cremation instead of burial. But once again, China's administrators were compelled to retain some ancient customs. The peasants were allowed to venerate their ancestors' memories. They were permitted to take flowers to their graves at the Ching Ming festival. And if families wished, they could bury their dead, provided the bodies were interred in rugged mountain terrain.

Chinese funerals, with traditional dancing and burnt offerings, were discouraged. Instead, families were advised to conduct secular "memory meetings" at the cremation grounds. Relatives and friends played music and listened to a short eulogy recited by someone representing the commune or the deceased's work group or factory.

The younger members of the commune had not been exposed to many religious or superstitious traditions, but the older peasants continued to adhere to some ancient practices. Lo Chin-loung, whose life was neatly bisected by history, twenty-four years before 1949 and twenty-four years since, still wore a translucent jade bracelet, a traditional Chinese source of good luck.

"I bought it when I got married," she recalled. "In the old society, people wanted them, but I didn't understand why."

Nevertheless, she wore it faithfully.

*   *   *

Another substantial rural tradition to survive the coming of the CCP
was the five-day market, one of the greatest anomalies at Kwang Li. Of
all the institutions in this controlled economy, none seemed more out
of place than this agricultural trade market, held every fifth morning
in Kwang Li town. But the existence of a "free" market of exchange
reaffirmed the tangible strain of pragmatism that was so much an
essential facet of Communism, Chinese-style.

On market days, dozens of elderly peasants with parchment-like skin
and floppy straw hats would bring poultry or produce to sell on the dirt
floor of the same amphitheater that accommodated sports competitions
and political rallies. As they assembled their bamboo cages of fowl and
stacked shiny cucumbers and ripe tomatoes in appetizing pyramids, a
cacophony of squawking birds and spirited chatter bubbled up the stone
steps from the sunken amphitheater and shattered the early morning
stillness. The peasants circulated around the rim of the enclosure,
surveying each other's goods and negotiating purchases. On market
days, it appeared as though the commune shed its mantle of socialism
to don temporarily the cloak of free enterprise.

The Kwang Li market was held every fifth day, and it had been for
as long as anyone could remember. Many of the colorful aspects of the
traditional Chinese market remained, reflecting one of the oldest established forms of commerce in the world. That included bartering and
haggling over a few pennies until a deal was consummated. Aged
peasants would hurl bids and counterproposals at each other. The
debate would continue, even after the buyer dipped a gnarled hand into
a frayed sack and produced a handful of crumpled banknotes and
assorted coins, until at last both parties grudgingly conceded.

The commune supply and marketing cooperative supervised the market, which welcomed all comers. But since participants usually had to
sacrifice at least a half-day's quota of work-points to attend the market,
most of the marketgoers were the elderly and retired who had time to
spare. Many toted grandchildren strapped to their backs, the children's
tiny heads secured in hand-sewn fishnet hats.

All the goods came from the peasants' private plots or backyards.
Many of the peasants in attendance, like chicken merchant Yeh Liu,
were market habitués. Yeh, whose hands and face were withered like
desiccated leaves, considered her occupation "caring for my four grandchildren." She regularly took the 2½-cents ferry-boat ride from her

Kwang Li's market in the town amphitheater.

The market reflected one of the oldest established forms of commerce in the world.

Marketgoers bartered and haggled over prices until a deal was consummated.

native village across the West River every two or three weeks to attend Kwang Li's trade fair.

Yeh said she consumed most of the vegetables she grew in her private plot, but since she raised about fifty chickens and geese, she usually had several to sell at the market. Today she had just sold a pair of loudly protesting chickens for $2.50 and was considering spending the proceeds on a fresh fish.

"Sometimes I spend all the money I earn here," she said.

Market transactions were not totally free. To "control capitalistic tendencies," Liang Wei-ming explained, the commune imposed a two-hour time limit on the market. Besides, he interjected, since all the goods were products of the private plots, and since the plots themselves were restricted in area, the amount each person could trade would never be excessive. The market, Liang summarized, was "just a convenience for exchanging goods."

Our official commune hosts assured us that itinerant peddlers no longer existed in the countryside. But Lu Mu-shen, a sixty-year-old dog merchant, traveled from another commune to sell his tiny caramel-colored puppies which, he told us, were intended as pets, although dogs were traditionally consumed as a delicacy. Crouching on the ground and bobbing his head to passers-by, Lu gladly demonstrated the health of his four-dollar pups by prying open their tiny jaws and revealing the flick of pink tongues. He picked up the dogs, letting their legs flop, then set them down and rubbed their furry necks affectionately.

In the CCP system, there was no provision for the wandering peddler. But we had found one, which meant that in the vast expanses of China there were cracks in the system that permitted idiosyncrasies.

Every circus has its clown, and the Kwang Li market did as well. Flashing his toothless grin, Lung Liang, a wild snake peddler who had spent all of his sixty years in a village of Kwang Li, kept the crowd in stitches with responses to the questions posed by we city slickers.

"Do you have to feed them?" we asked naïvely, as he untied the strings of a dirt-stained bag and let his snakes coil in the open air.

"It's not necessary," he replied balefully. "They've eaten enough *before* I catch them."

As the reptiles entwined around each other and the spectators pressed forward expectantly, Lung explained that he supported himself by selling his snakes for a dollar or two each.

Most of the marketgoers were the elderly who had time to spare.

Nobody seemed surprised to hear that someone who practiced this arcane profession lived alone.

"Do they bite?" we asked, feeding the snake man another straight line.

"Oh, yes," he replied, shaking his closely sheared head at the ignorance of these foreign devils, "but I keep plenty of medicine at home." He chortled, and the crowd snickered along with him.

The market was not only one of the last vestiges of capitalism for country dwellers, it was a major source of entertainment as well.

The black market that flourished at Kwang Li provided another surprising dimension to the inconsistencies of life on the commune. The emigrant in Hong Kong described the black market and told us the commune authorities knew of its operations but closed their eyes to them, since the volume of such trade was insignificant.

In fact, he said the peasants engaged in black market trading right under the cadres' eyes at the five-day market, selling small remnants of pork left over from their personal consumption. He said that only those peasants who raised pigs were entitled to pork rationing coupons, which they obtained along with cash when they sold their pigs for slaughter. The coupons, equivalent to about 40 percent of the sale, could be traded for pork at a controlled price of about 80 cents per pound. But if the peasants could not consume all this meat themselves, or if they preferred having some extra cash, they could sell the pork at black market prices. The refugee recalled that prices fluctuated at about $1.90 a pound—over twice as much as the regulated price. Only when such trading became a "regular business," he said, would commune officials interfere.

The refugee described a black market in several other items, such as peanut oil for cooking, which was rationed to members of production teams that did not produce enough peanuts. Teams which grew sufficient peanuts needed no coupons to purchase oil.

Rice was also traded on the black market. Selling rice was a covert enterprise, more stealthy than the meat trade. The emigrant said a peasant who wished to sell food grain illegally would take a sack of unhusked rice from his home and proceed as if he were going to the rice mill to have the husks removed. When a potential customer approached him, the peasant would hand over the bag of rice to the purchaser, who would simply carry the newly bought grain to the mill himself. Black market rice fetched an even higher price proportionately than pork: The state-controlled price was $4.45 per hundred pounds of third-grade rice, but the black market price reached as high as $12, $13, or even $14 for the same amount of rice. The emigrant said the cadres knew about this illicit trade, but they did not ordinarily meddle in it, since it was plainly "between individuals."

13
THE SEXES

"Before Liberation," recalled forty-eight-year-old Lo Chin-loung in her singsong Cantonese, "if a boy's family could afford it, he would go to school. But a girl never would.

"When the men talked with each other, the women would sit aside. We would never join in. If they called a meeting, the women would never sit with the men. We had to sit aside and keep silent while the men chatted."

Lo drew a long breath and smiled faintly.

"Now," she continued, with evident pride, "we are all equal. Now we sit together, and we talk with the men."

In Asia, China pioneered in many areas of women's rights; and the new image of unfettered, emancipated Chinese peasant women was painted and sung by propagandists and journalists. In fact, many other nations could probably learn from the Chinese experience.

But after taking a closer look at the women's role in Kwang Li, we were disappointed to find persistent contradictions.

When viewed in the overall context of Chinese history—those long centuries when Chinese peasant women were considered as little more than chattel—the status of contemporary women had improved. The women of Kwang Li judged their present status from this perspective. In fairness, perhaps foreigners should view them that way, too: against a backdrop of countless generations of oppression, with only a few, recent moments of opportunity.

But in the land of "Liberation," equality of the sexes was often illusory, and injustices remained.

Chinese women were officially liberated in 1950, when the revised marriage law obliterated the major sex-oriented injustices of the past in one legal stroke. The law banned such common practices as arranged or forced marriages and endowed women with the rights to own and inherit property, to divorce, and to remarry after divorce or widowhood. At the same time, women were theoretically given the right to earn "equal pay for equal work," and government propaganda began to assault attitudes that tolerated inequality based on sexual discrimination, which had persisted longer in the countryside than in the cities.

Laws rarely eradicate ingrained beliefs or traditional practices overnight, but progress had been encouraging.

With women's rights, as with many other areas of commune life, the CCP attempted to prohibit harmful traditions but refrained from interfering in many innocuous customs. So, marriage remained sacrosanct.

Previously, arranged marriages were common among wealthy, urban Chinese; but they were also not unknown among the peasants of Kwang Li. Today, though newlyweds Hsieh Ping and Chen Siu-yang (of the poor-peasant Chen family) met through parental introduction, they courted for three years and decided to marry *before* soliciting their parents' approval.

"First we got acquainted. Then we fell in love," recalled the bridegroom, Chen, unabashedly.

"I proposed to Hsieh Ping outside my house. *Then* I asked my mother, and she said, 'Good.' "

The emigrant in Hong Kong, who was single, recalled that most Kwang Li couples met through go-betweens; and he told us, "There were very few cases of free romance." He said unmarried young men and women rarely conversed with one another.

But he also noted, "I never saw a case of marriage dictated by parents' orders."

Commune officials claimed that they questioned both applicants before issuing marriage certificates, to ensure that the wedding was not compulsory and that polygamy or concubinage were not involved. Marriage licenses cost about 5 cents, and no legal vows were necessary. In fact, the couple's parents usually performed the marriage ceremony by saying a few words at a family gathering.

In the CCP view, commune weddings should only be simple celebrations, where friends and relatives assembled at the home of the new couple to wish them well and sometimes play pranks, such as throwing firecrackers or demanding that the groom sing a song—Chinese versions of old shoes and tin cans.

Accordingly, when Hsieh Ping and Chen Siu-yang were married in front of about thirty family members and friends, they served village fare: chicken, duck, goose, pork, and wine; and the young husband presented cakes and candies, customary matrimonial gifts, to his bride's parents. The entire wedding, including their new furniture, cost only about $100. There were no wedding rings, an unheard-of luxury in rural China.

Nevertheless, the emigrant from Kwang Li reported instances of "extravagant" wedding banquets on the commune, and brigade surveyor Chen Chi-fun, a middle peasant, admitted spending nearly one-half of his family's annual income on his son's marriage.

The peasant marriage of Hsieh Ping and Chen Siu-yang would have been considered exemplary from the CCP point of view, except for the fact that the couple was so young: both only twenty-two. China's leaders have encouraged marriage in the mid- and late twenties; but in rural areas like this commune, with purportedly free courtship and plenty of wide-open rice fields, it was difficult to enforce this principle.

Although Chinese women could now file for divorce, free choice in marriage and long-established custom kept divorce at Kwang Li to a minimum. Commune officials could only recall two cases since 1968. The commune headquarters assigned a cadre to supervise marriage problems and maintained a marriage tribunal; but in case of divorce, the county court made the final decision.

Because it entitled women to share the common ownership, management, and inheritance of family possessions, the marriage law had far-reaching implications in eroding the traditional patriarchy. Women at Kwang Li talked proudly of family possessions, which partly belonged to them. Even after divorce, a woman legally had rights to that property which was hers before marriage; and mutual household goods were to be divided.

As Chinese newlyweds have done for thousands of years, Hsieh Ping and her husband lived with his parents, the poor peasant Chens. To them, this was not evidence of male domination. Convenience outweighed the advantages of privacy, and presumably Hsieh Ping would be grateful for her mother-in-law's assistance and babysitting services when Hsieh started raising a family.

Neither this wide-eyed bride nor her slender, sinewy husband complained about living with his parents.

"We would not like to live separately," said the young wife, squatting

Hsieh Ping's husband and father-in-law prepare lunch.

on her doorstep. "We are used to doing things this way."

Nevertheless, the tales of pre-1949 Chinese mothers-in-law abusing and even driving their daughters-in-law to suicide prompted inquiries about the division of housework in Hsieh's family. Everyone, she reported brightly, pitched in when he or she had time. Usually her mother-in-law did the cooking. But the Chinese considered cooking a skilled job, and Hsieh's husband and father-in-law occasionally helped prepare meals. Even while we talked on the doorstep, the men of this household were preparing lunch, and the aroma of cooking-oil and frying fish wafted from the old house that the Chens used as a kitchen. Hsieh Ping said she usually washed dishes, scrubbed the floors, gathered and chopped pig fodder, and carried water. In *her* family home, she said her sister-in-law performed similar chores.

Hsieh Ping described the relationship with her mother-in-law as quite amicable; but the emigrant from Kwang Li told us later that mothers-in-law often quarreled with their sons' wives about housework.

Hsieh's husband, who joined her on the stoop after moistening his neck with a towel, insisted that both he and his wife took turns carrying buckets of water from the village well.

"There's no timetable," he explained, laughing affectionately.

But usually, when we heard the sloshing of water, it was Hsieh, and not her husband, hunched under the weight of the shoulder-yoke, gliding along with two buckets of well water.

"Before getting married, I never asked how much money I earned," Hsieh Ping said apologetically, squinting slightly in the midday sunlight. "My mother received my salary, and I asked her for spending money. I don't even know how many work-points I earned then. Since I was married, I do know what I earn. I have an 'A' rating."

Hsieh said she contributed her pay check to her husband's family, but she could draw upon it when she wished.

The city-bred emigrant in Hong Kong concluded that, on the commune, "women's lot is much more bitter" than that of men. Peasant women, he recalled, arose at 4:00 A.M. to cook pig fodder and prepare the family's breakfast. Aside from fertilizing the family land plot, the men rarely performed domestic chores such as laundry, he said. The same applied to children, although the emigrant reported young boys helped "quite a bit" around the house. He said the bulk of children's domestic duties, such as cutting firewood and mountain grass, cooking,

Newlywed Hsieh Ping at the village well.

and washing vegetables, fell upon the girls.

Commune members easily justified these contradictions to their professed sexual equality.

Hsieh Ping's mother-in-law put it pragmatically, "Frankly, in our production brigade, women do more housework than men. But the men do the heavy work."

It was more difficult to rationalize a similar formula applied to daily farm work. Although she was a top-grade "A" worker, Hsieh Ping did not have the opportunity to earn as much money as a man. What's more, she spent her days cultivating crops in a work group composed entirely of women.

Kwang Li's division of labor by sex revealed that China's much-publicized "equal pay for equal work" principle was not always honored in practice. Huang Lien-tsi, a twenty-three-year-old commune women's department worker who accompanied us on many interviews, said that the commune usually segregated men and women because their physical capacities were different and because same-sex groups "work more closely together and get better results."

She pointed out that by emphasizing the achievements of all-female teams, the commune could demonstrate women's singular contributions.

But sexually segregating work groups kept incomes separate and unequal. Since they were deemed physically weaker, women were assigned less vigorous tasks. Men plowed, while women weeded the crops; men carried fertilizer, women scattered it. A job such as tending fruit trees went to a man, while caring for water buffaloes was a female assignment. What made this system unequal was that the more arduous tasks carried more work-points per day. Women, who weeded the fields (a thirteen-work-points job) and could not haul rocks (a man's job, worth fifteen work-points), were thus systematically barred from earning a man's income.

Far from receiving equal pay for equal work, the commune's female labor force generally earned less pay for different work.

The situation was reflected in the pay check of Chang Hui-chun, a twenty-eight-year-old top-grade field laborer whose husband earned more than twice as much as she did. Chang was a pudgy-cheeked woman with hair sheared to the contours of an inverted mixing-bowl. Her legs were encased in a film of mud that splattered the knee-high cuffs of her rolled-up blue trousers, as she paused from her rice-growing chores to discuss her salary.

At the end of 1972, Chang reported, she received $175, plus 825 pounds of food grain, and items such as fish, which she had purchased on credit. Together, her two children were allotted about 770 pounds of food grain for the year.

But, in the same year, her husband, also an agricultural worker, earned twice as much, $350, plus nearly 900 pounds of rice.

"He transports heavy goods," explained Chang with a smile, rationalizing why her husband earned twenty work-points a day while she only averaged ten. But she acknowledged that even when she performed similar vigorous jobs, she only received fifteen work-points.

These apparent injustices did not seem to bother the women of Kwang Li. Men engaged in heavier physical work, the women argued, so they *should* earn more. Besides, during the busy seasons, women could tackle the same tasks as men—transplanting and harvesting— which merited an equivalent fifteen work-points.

"That," pronounced women's department worker Huang, as if to settle the matter, "is 'equal pay for equal work.' "

Men also dominated commune politics. Peasant women regularly attended neighborhood women's meetings and political discussions. But getting the women to participate in political sessions was not easy for commune leaders. At one study meeting, we waited while half-a-dozen male speakers commented before one woman spoke out.

Sometimes commune administrators did not even bother to maintain a facade of equal representation. Poor-peasant Lo Chin-loung's neighborhood production team had only two female leaders out of twelve. But, Lo observed, "Men do the heavier work, so they need more spokesmen. As long as we have at least one representative, the *number* of women isn't important."

Even though women outnumbered men on the production brigade committee in Lo's village, the females were relegated to supervising youth groups and women's work, while the males handled hard-nosed administrative jobs with broader responsibilities.

When women were consigned to minority status at higher levels of commune government, this phenomenon was not as easy to rationalize. Only one female member served on the Revolutionary Committee running the commune. And, despite her important rank in the women's department, whenever we chatted with male administrators, Huang Lien-tsi inevitably poured tea.

To farm women, living in remote villages where equality was only an abstract concept, such contradictions were probably irrelevant. What were important to them were the more fundamental changes the CCP had dictated, especially the marriage law, which by fiat had changed the course of the peasant women's lives.

Young commune females now had the same opportunity as the males to receive an education. In just about equal numbers, boys and girls occupied the ranks of Kwang Li's schools, although the emigrant in Hong Kong said that after third grade, children were segregated. At Kwang Li, there was also a watershed among the teachers. There were more female instructors in the primary grades, while more males taught the upper classes.

For young men, the process of growing up in Kwang Li had changed in the years since 1949, though not as dramatically as for their female counterparts.

Despite the marriage law, the countryside remained a male-dominated society. Men ran their households. They controlled property rights, except in rare instances where families had no male heirs or in cases of divorce. For the most part, families also aspired to conceiving male offspring.

The emigrant from Kwang Li reported that men from his production team regularly spent their evenings in conversation with other men. Often they would share the evening meal with their neighbors. The men had a fondness for gambling, and when the day's work was done, poker was their favorite pastime.

These activities were exclusively male. The men even stayed awake longer to talk among themselves. The women would retire earlier, since their domestic chores began earlier in the day.

China's new society functioned within stringent limits—travel restrictions, no freedom to seek employment elsewhere, and only one narrow avenue of political thought. But the militarism that suffused rural Chinese life did not seem so ominous when we realized that just as in wartime, China during the 1950s had faced a dire emergency. As if they were calling up the whole nation to rise in arms against an enemy, the CCP leaders had drafted the entire Chinese people to confront their economic problems. Individual communities had never before possessed the resources or the organization to achieve security and prosperity. So, although China's authoritarian atmosphere seemed oppressive to outsiders, this highly structured system had also enabled the Chinese people to achieve success where chaos reigned before.

Ambition was constrained, in the controlled society of the commune, but the favorite goal of many young people was a career in the People's Liberation Army. The commune boasted it could field a militia of ten thousand peasants, and many of the younger members applied to join the PLA.

The army had been romanticized in song and story since 1949, and it was the vanguard of the Cultural Revolution; so its appeal was natural, even though only a handful of commune youth were likely to be accepted into its ranks.

Perhaps the most revolutionary change in the countryside was the new attitude concerning children and family size. In the old society, as in most of Southeast Asia today, families would strive for as many male children as possible, even bearing half a dozen or more daughters until at last a son was born. But we realized that Chinese views had shifted radically when poor-peasant Lo Chin-loung told us that two children were enough for one woman, and when she added that, although the best combination was one boy and one girl, she would not object to two girls.

Hsieh Ping, the newlywed, was well-versed in the family planning advice with which young Chinese were constantly bombarded. Smiling in flushed embarrassment, the young bride said she would like to limit her future offspring to two; and she hoped to wait at least three years after marriage before having her first child. More than two children, she asserted, would be harmful to her health. Besides, she said, a large family was no longer necessary. She was referring to the ancient practice of relying on children to till the family soil and to provide the parents' future security, even when real security was only a fantasy for most Chinese.

The emigrant in Hong Kong recalled that Kwang Li leaders started advocating birth control strongly in 1972. At that time, he said, production team officials threatened that couples having over three children might not receive household registration and grain rations.

Subsequently, Kwang Li officials claimed, their local population growth rate hovered near the national ideal at 2.1 percent each year.

Peasant midwives in the villages distributed contraceptives, usually a combination of Western devices and Chinese herbal medicines, to any women who requested them. When we asked Hsieh Ping if this included unmarried women, the only reply this young country woman would give was to giggle shyly. The interpreter hurriedly assured us that, "of course," unmarried women could not obtain such things.

Though the commune made available most forms of contraception including sterilization, birth control pills were the most popular method; and Hsieh Ping said she had never heard of any alternatives. She talked of a once-a-month pill, which she and her neighbors had been taking on an experimental basis for over one year. A surgeon at the commune hospital confirmed this report, though he could not locate complete statistics for the commune experiments, nor could he produce a sample capsule. The stock had run out, he explained lamely.

The commune also had the medical capability of sterilizing its male residents, but the emigrant from Kwang Li said he had not heard of such a practice. He said that in reality, no matter how many offspring commune men had fathered, they still worried they might not have sufficient male heirs to carry on the family line.

Although the women's loose-fitting clothing was concealing, there did not seem to be any pregnant women on the streets and in the fields of Kwang Li People's Commune. We asked why. We learned that after the first months of pregnancy, women stayed home and performed lighter chores such as drying straw in the sunlight, for which they received their ordinary quota of work-points. Childbirth usually took place in the home, assisted by a trained midwife, using equipment sterilized in a hospital or dispensary. Only a few decades ago, the commune-dwellers recalled, midwives used to deliver babies with only a broken piece of porcelain for a surgical instrument.

Women at Kwang Li received paid sick leave: fifty-six days for maternity cases and twelve days for abortions. Commune doctors described abortion as a last resort, urging women to rely on prevention first. But women who requested abortions received them at the commune hospital—and as with childbirth care, at a minimal cost. In a three-month period in 1973, doctors at Kwang Li's hospital said that sixty women, most of them married, underwent abortions.

Elaborate fashions never had their place in the rice fields. Before 1949 peasant women worried about having enough to eat, instead of about having something pretty to wear. Only the wealthy wives and concubines in the cities dressed in silks and used cosmetics. Today, though the villagers were more secure, there were still higher priorities than fashion. But pragmatism did not keep the peasant women from looking neat and attractive.

Along with the famous baggy trousers, we spotted some mildly fashionable trappings. Fashionable, that is, by Chinese standards.

With her "trousseau" wardrobe of twenty flowered or patterned blouses, five pairs of trousers, and five pairs of shoes, mostly open-toed sandals, Hsieh Ping was a well-dressed peasant bride. Not only that, but her apparel was economical. She pointed to her blue trousers, which cost only a few dollars to make, and to her home-sewn flowered shirt.

"Young women like the flowered patterns," she said, commenting pragmatically that "patterned cloth doesn't cost any more than plain material."

At work, women covered their blouses with navy blue aprons sprinkled with gaily-colored embroidered flowers. During moments of relaxation, there was time for attention to appearance. Peasant women plucked each other's facial hairs with makeshift tweezers fashioned from string. They even wore a favorite hairstyle, pulling their bangs through a plastic comb and tying them in a short ponytail that flopped at the top of their heads.

"For several years, we have worn our hair this way," said the poor-peasant Chens' twenty-two-year-old daughter-in-law, a squad leader in the women's militia, as she stitched a pair of pajamas on the family sewing machine.

"We prefer this style, since it is comfortable," she said. "The comb on the top holds the hair back when we are working. We fasten it at the back of our heads with ribbons of all colors, but many prefer red."

Just why the peasant women chose red hair ribbons *en masse* she would not say. But we detected a utilitarian peasant *chic* that was as much a part of daily life at Kwang Li as Chairman Mao's picture.

Kwang Li's administrative committee operated an active women's department, which conducted meetings at least once a month in the villages. In China, women's liberation was official policy, so feminist leaders like the tomboyish Huang Lien-tsi were employed by the government and received the salaries of cadres.

Huang was a sturdy, somewhat dour woman with a gravelly voice. Pigtails sprouted from a crooked part that meandered over her scalp. Her brusque manner indicated that she had little time for frivolity.

Feminist Huang Lien-tsi.

Huang said she became interested in women's rights at sixteen, shortly after graduation from junior middle school, when she began work in the small commune starch factory. Most of the employees were women, not an unusual phenomenon in China, where same-sex industries were traditional. From her fellow employees, she told us, she learned the importance and problems of the female labor force.

Because she was active in political discussions, the factory women's group elected Huang as a "leading member" of their association. Five years later, in March 1972, she was chosen to work in the commune women's department. She said she did not apply but was assigned to the job.

Huang, who had only completed seven years of education, said she had no expectation of continuing her studies. When she left school, China was in the throes of the Cultural Revolution and there was no hope of graduating to higher education. Now, at twenty-three, she rationalized, she was too old. But she remarked complacently that she had no regrets, for she could make greater progress through "practical knowledge."

We sensed that this was a flimsy rationalization, since her words flowed almost too assuredly. In fact, Huang had no choice about her future, and so she was resigned to making the most of her situation.

Huang explained she would acquire a practical education through three types of experiences outlined by Chairman Mao and his disciples. First, studying on her own would enable her to learn about China and to raise her personal cultural standards. Next, from her work in the factory and in the fields during her required sixty days' labor, she was learning firsthand about production. Finally, even on a rural commune, she had the opportunity to conduct simple experiments.

In this way, said Huang confidently, "I can learn more than I could learn in three years or more in the classroom."

Already, while employed in the factory, she had attempted to make glucose from cassava starch and to convert discarded industrial water into fertilizer.

"It may not be the most advanced research in the world or even in our country," she said philosophically, "but in a small village like ours, we must do things ourselves."

Huang was curious about women's liberation movements in the United States and elsewhere, but she was disappointed to learn that foreigners often criticized Chinese women for their drab appearance. In

Chinese society, baggy trousers and pigtails were not considered unattractive.

"After all," said Huang, tossing her braids, "we always dressed like this in the countryside, where we have always been poor. We are still constructing our country, so we cannot spend too much time and money on beauty, nor do we want to."

She added with a smile, "Remember, our way of life is different from yours. Our women devote their energy to production, and this is what they think is best."

Huang spent most of her time in the remote areas of the commune's mountainous terrain, conducting a Chinese form of women's liberation meetings. Apparently attendance was not required, for one young farmer mentioned that she was more active in coeducational activities.

Huang Lien-tsi, who led some discussion groups, said the need for special pep talks stemmed from the importance of women.

"You see," explained Huang earnestly, wrinkling her freckled nose, "Chairman Mao has said, 'Women support half the heaven.' "

Huang admitted another purpose of these gatherings was to correct outdated attitudes, such as women's reluctance to assume political leadership. She said she used the meetings to pass on official requests to the women, to solicit their requests and to urge women to participate more actively in collective labor.

Sometimes the topics at women's gatherings stressed the positive. Discussion leaders like Huang enumerated the benefits the CCP brought Chinese women. They reviewed the lives of heroines and discussed how to learn from their examples. Elderly women described how they had suffered in the old society, and how fortunate they were now.

But the need for such discussions indicated that the commune leaders were not entirely satisfied with the women's performance and that they felt it necessary to maintain a forum to encourage women to air complaints.

After repeated questioning, Huang finally acknowledged that deep-rooted problems still existed in the Chinese countryside in the form of "incorrect thinking" among both men and women, particularly those who grew up before 1949.

"Incorrect thinking," she observed, was reflected in the disdain shown by elderly men, who were educated before the CCP era, toward their wives, who were often illiterate.

Surprisingly, when pressed, Huang admitted, "This incorrect thinking is more serious among women." She cited older women's tendency to remain passive in leadership roles. But in Huang's view, women's reticence did not represent as serious a problem as, say, if they had refrained from working.

Other discussion themes emphasized women's potential. By encouraging women to perform experiments in farming, the women's department highlighted female contributions. Acclaim was especially necessary, Huang pointed out, because formerly Chinese men did not consider women capable of conducting scientific research.

For their part, peasant women used the meetings to deliver their complaints to commune headquarters. Usually they asked for help in political organization or similar matters. Illiteracy, more prevalent among women, was a problem commune officials believed could best be tackled in a female context; so, when women asked for reading lessons, the commune responded with free classes for women. Some older, illiterate women also asked the women's workers to tell them about current events. Huang Lien-tsi insisted that the women did not confront her with more serious grievances.

Finally, to ensure that the female members of Kwang Li's community accepted their new status and responsibilities, Huang and her department carried on a continuing propaganda campaign. They exhorted women to join the labor force and reminded them of women's role in Communist history.

In a society where both men and women were constantly reminded of their communal obligations, such campaigns might seem superfluous; but the women's department did not want to take any chances that the message was not getting through, and the CCP recognized the value of spreading their message on a woman-to-woman basis.

"China is a developing country," asserted Huang Lien-tsi, "so we still have to mobilize everyone to work.

"But," she added triumphantly, "the emancipation of women is not a temporary measure."

14
EDUCATION

"I am a people's soldier on guard by the ocean.
I love the blue ocean
Because it's beside the motherland.
To defend the motherland,
I'll fight with unceasing effort."

Even ten-year-olds at Kwang Li learned about politics. The second-grade primary school students who sang this song in music class had never seen the ocean. Nor did they fully understand what it meant to defend their country. But they were taught early in life about military discipline.

Every day when the school bell signaled the end of a drowsy morning of lesson-chanting in Sui Kang production brigade's school, a public address system blared out a stirring musical refrain. Children filed onto the school's basketball court, where they fell in, forming parallel lines. They stood at attention, their hands pressed to their sides. Then, in four-quarter time, still in formation, the neighborhood "squads" marched home for lunch.

The atmosphere was less martial during preschool years. Commune youngsters grew up enveloped in love and attention. While their parents worked, grandparents cared for most small children, toting them on their backs or bouncing them on their knees, just as they had done for centuries.

Before children were seven or eight and enrolled in school, there was not much organized activity. Some of the production brigades organized day-care centers—modestly furnished one-room schools where village women taught small children to read and write simple characters.

But facilities were primitive, and in one dusty village courtyard, we

School dismissal resembled a military drill.

watched as a group of children and their teacher passed the afternoon slapping playing cards on the ground in a spirited Kwang Li version of "Crazy Eights."

Many children had household responsibilities thrust upon them as soon as they could walk. They cared for younger brothers and sisters and carried them papoose-style as they wandered the village streets looking for amusement. These youngsters resourcefully converted just about any objects—including tools and household utensils—into playthings.

The best cared-for preschoolers at Kwang Li were the 125 children enrolled in the commune's only kindergarten. They were the sons and daughters of factory and administration workers. During working hours, their parents left the kindergarteners in a sprawling one-story cement building adjacent to Kwang Li town.

These tots were a fortunate few. For about $2.60 a year, they could spend their days cavorting at miniature Ping-Pong tables and rocking horses, jumping rope, playing basketball, and singing songs to the accompaniment of a foot-pedal organ.

Children in the kindergarten wore the cleanest and most colorful clothes on the commune. The girls bounded through the steps of their games in full skirts and embroidered blouses; they all sported red hair ribbons. The boys wore striped or colored T-shirts.

Once they started first grade, though, most commune children entered a more restrained routine. In the villages, each production brigade ran and financed its own five-year primary and two-year junior middle school, under the aegis of the county education department. Although education was not compulsory, commune officials claimed that all but a few children attended at least primary school.

A few parents kept their children at home to contribute to the family farm income. Perhaps they felt the school was too far from home. Some families possibly did not trust the schools.

Chen Su-ching, the pert ten-year-old daughter of the middle-peasant Chens, attended primary school in Sui Kang production brigade. Chen, who had a heart-shaped face, liked playing Ping-Pong and hide-and-seek. Like any sanguine youngster her age, she spent her allowance on candy. Chen wore the red bandanna of the Little Red Soldiers, an honorary society. When she had started school at age nine, she had been selected for this elite group. Once known as the Young Pioneers, the Little Red Soldiers were being trained as China's future leaders. Their

Not all the schoolwork was repetitious lesson-chanting.

teachers chose about half the students in Chen's school for this group on the basis of their performance in their studies and physical training.

The Little Red Soldiers offered a surprising contradiction within a system we had expected to be based on impartiality. Through their school years, the commune's good students were constantly singled out for attention. A kindergarten teacher proudly identified her best student, and a high school English instructor repeatedly called upon the same handful of students to answer questions.

Chen Su-ching's basic curriculum resembled that of primary school children all over the world. By the time she finished seven years of school, she would have studied Chinese, mathematics, physics, chemistry, English, drawing, sports, and music. In addition, she would complete a course in agriculture and industry, which combined theory with practical training in raising crops, selecting various strains of plants, fertilizing fields, and field management, as well as such industrial techniques as ironmongering.

Classes were conducted in Mandarin or *p'u t'ung hua,* the national language, which the children learned in addition to their regional dialect, Cantonese. Music lessons served to introduce the youngest pupils to the official tongue.

A large proportion of Chen Su-ching's education was devoted to the thought (writings) of CCP Chairman Mao Tse-tung and to other political teachings. As she learned to read and practiced simple arithmetic, Chen also studied how to "serve the people" and "distribute energies for socialist construction."

Her classes were large, often with as many as forty children. She spent seven hours a day in class and averaged half an hour of homework a night. In the higher grades, the assignments would increase to one hour nightly.

Children at Kwang Li took three sets of examinations a year and were graded for "morality" and "intellectual and physical condition" as well as academic achievement. Everyone passed to the next grade; exceptional children were rewarded with certificates or prizes, and slow learners were assigned tutors.

These rural Chinese students practiced a form of democracy. At an annual class meeting, Chen Su-ching and her schoolmates elected their own class committee. Each committee member fulfilled a special responsibility, such as monitor, or committee member in charge of sports or physical labor.

Education was inexpensive—only about $1 for Chen's tuition and about $2 for her books, every year. These low tariffs, and the convenient location of the village schools, provided what the government called universal education, available to virtually every young person in China today. Although the quality of their education lagged behind Western standards, the Chinese peasant youngsters had access to learning and literacy, something which many of their counterparts in several subsistence-level Asian societies still do not enjoy.

"I had a very hard time when I was young," Chen Su-ching's mother said pensively, as she carried dishes to the kitchen. "I could not afford school, so I only went for one year; and I only learned to read some very simple characters.

"In the old days, I never thought of going to school . . . never. And I never thought of my children going to school.

"Now, things have changed, and all my children will be educated."

Although Chen Su-ching and her thirteen-year-old brother said they expected to finish junior middle school, their mother said she would not compel them to complete the production brigade's seven-year-course.

"It will be up to them to decide," she asserted. "When they want to go to work, they can."

In the countryside, few children advanced beyond the normal seven-year village education. But Kwang Li was one of the few rural communes in China with its own two-year senior middle school. Space at this school was limited to three hundred fifty, and the headmaster said that the school turned away half its applicants every year.

Administered by the commune and financed by the county government, which paid operating costs and teachers' salaries, the senior middle school functioned similarly to the production brigade schools with respect to class democracy, grading, and curriculum. Most of the senior middle school teachers were graduates of teachers' training college in Canton; they received an average wage of $29 a month.

The senior middle school cost slightly more than the village schools, about $3 a year for tuition and $1 for books. Since the school was located in Kwang Li town, one hundred students from far-off villages roomed free of charge at a dormitory, paying $5 a month for food.

Beginning in early childhood, peer pressure was normally applied to obtain compliance. So teachers at this school claimed they had no serious disciplinary problems, and that their most common grievance was absenteeism.

Elaborate recreational facilities were low-priority items in China's scheme of education. The fourteen- and fifteen-year-olds at Kwang Li's senior middle school had to be content with such simple sporting equipment as Ping-Pong tables and outdoor basketball. But this rudimentary athletic program was still a vast improvement over much of Asia. The school also planned picnics once or twice a year and held camping trips. Other school outings included trips to neighboring people's communes to listen to the poor peasants' stories about the hardships of life before 1949.

At senior middle school, as in all Kwang Li's educational institutions, the influence of politics was profound. Political teaching became even more pervasive after the Cultural Revolution, which swept the country in the late 1960s, shaking the foundations of China's educational system.

Daily life at Kwang Li continued relatively undisturbed throughout the course of the Cultural Revolution, but the first tremors of the nationwide movement to reach this commune resounded in the schools, and there the repercussions have been the most spectacular.

Some schools shut down in 1967 for an entire year so that the students and many of their teachers could travel and participate in "revolutionary experiences." The young people and teachers staged "struggle meetings" to denounce local and national leaders. They also organized Red Guard units to influence politics and industry and to re-enact the Long March of the Red Army in 1934–1935. They criticized and attempted to eradicate what were described as "manifestations of feudal culture," such as Buddhist temples; and they formed Mao Tse-tung Thought Propaganda Teams to spread the Chairman's words through songs, dances, skits, and group readings. Some of these activities led to violence in China's major cities, but school officials said there was no violence at Kwang Li.

In 1967, prematurely white-haired Hsu Kuang-lin, age forty, had been head of the junior middle school in Kwang Li town, which was then the loftiest educational institution on the commune. The soft-spoken Hsu, who combined the casual good humor of a peasant with the dignity of an educator, did not accompany his students on their Cultural Revolution exploits, for, he explained, smiling, "someone had to look after the school."

Hsu recalled the 1967 period as a meaningful experience. He justified the sacrifice to education, claiming the student movement wiped out reactionary influence throughout Chinese society.

On their journeys, Hsu recounted, most of the Kwang Li students traveled only to Chao Ch'ing (Shiu Hing), the county seat, but some older students went as far as Canton in trips organized by the school and financed by the government. As the students traveled, they "linked up" with other schools, where they ate and slept.

Even those who did not leave home had plenty of opportunity for "revolutionary experience." Sometimes groups of students visited elderly peasants at Kwang Li and neighboring communes to hear their stories of pre-1949 suffering. Or the students would organize local propaganda teams to denounce the "reactionary" line of former head of state Liu Shao-chi.

The Cultural Revolution emphasized the importance of the peasants, who constitute about 80 percent of China's population. Chairman Mao apparently believed that some CCP leaders were ignoring the peasants, whom he identified as the foundation of China's basically agrarian society. So Mao exhorted young people to "consult" with the peasants, particularly the poor peasants who never owned land, and to discuss what their lives were like "before Liberation" (1949). Presumably, by "learning from the peasants," the activists in China—the educated youth, administrative cadres, CCP members, and others—would better understand the peasants' current problems and dedicate their efforts to solving them.

Not all the young people in the Kwang Li area actively participated in the Cultural Revolution. During that time, women's worker Huang Lien-tsi, who had already finished school, had helped her parents in the fishery production brigade; Tsin Han-chung, the factory lathe operator, said he had been "too young to understand what was going on."

After several months, headmaster Hsu reported, the students were trained in their "revolutionary struggle." Then, in 1968, they responded to Chairman Mao's call to reopen the schools.

Kwang Li's youth returned from their exploits to find many changes in the educational system. As part of a national campaign to concentrate more learning into less classroom time, the pre-Cultural Revolution six-year primary and three-year junior middle schools were condensed into a five-year primary course, followed by two years of junior middle school and, mainly in the cities, two years of senior middle school.

Since each of Kwang Li's twenty-one production brigades was now operating at least one primary and junior middle school, rather than just primary schools, more children were actually going to school longer than before.

Possibly because Kwang Li was designated as a model area, in 1968, Hsu's school began enrolling senior middle school students. The headmaster offered a different reason: He cited a growing demand for education from among the poor and lower-middle peasants, who previously had to send their children fifteen miles away to senior middle school if they were among the handful chosen for this privilege. Fortuitously, the "peasants' demands" coincided with Chairman Mao's exhortation at that time to keep peasant children as close as possible to the rice fields of home.

The Cultural Revolution also brought many changes in curriculum and school operations. As another device to stress the peasants' importance, local peasants were encouraged to recommend students for senior middle school, although the school also conducted qualifying examinations. English replaced Russian as the required foreign language, perhaps because of the heightened confrontation with the Soviet Union.

"Lesson sixteen. Read after me, ' barked the instructor in a regular English class of first-year senior middle school students.

"The sun is red!" boomed the voices of thirty young teenagers in unison. "The sun is bright! The sun is Chairman Mao!" they chanted in sing-song repetition.

"Chairman Mao is the red sun in our hearts!" they repeated, the words resounding off the walls. "We wish Chairman Mao a long, long life!"

Although the class memorized rote phrases, they could not understand our spoken English, and we needed an interpreter to talk with their teacher.

The senior middle school could not afford a reading room, but it maintained a lending library of about six hundred to seven hundred books. Headmaster Hsu confessed sorrowfully, none of the books were in English because "our standard is too low."

Even after the Cultural Revolution subsided, the educational revolution continued, as evidenced by the contents of a "blackboard magazine" in the senior middle schoolyard. Once or twice a week, the school's more artistically inclined students composed and illustrated chalk essays on such topics as Chinese literature, an honor roll, or an English lesson.

A typical school news bulletin indicated that these students continued to discuss the issues of the Cultural Revolution. The article "Comment on the Criticism and Repudiation of Liu Shao-chi's Revisionist Line" described how most students and teachers had actively criticized the policies of the former head of state.

A few blackboard essays were written in a lighter vein. One essay related an incident in which some students left their classroom in disarray after they made clay models, until several schoolmates volunteered to clean up the mess.

"We should learn from them," concluded the essayist.

The students were also encouraged to emulate a classmate who reportedly conducted research in his spare time to master the concept of electrical semiconductors, which he had failed to understand in class.

"It is the spirit of hard study; everyone must learn from him," sermonized the writer.

Another student who found a purse containing money and a fountain pen and returned it to its owner, was cited as a laudable example of good citizenship.

During the Cultural Revolution, the students' experiences initiated a continuous, introspective political process that remained a dominant factor in school life.

Another outgrowth of the Cultural Revolution was a Mao directive entrusting the leadership of Kwang Li's schools to the poorer peasants. The CCP apparently hoped peasant guidance would inevitably set the children upon a "correct," revolutionary course, a path that would prevent the growth of an inbred intellectual elite and keep the younger generation from forgetting what the "Great Proletarian Cultural Revolution" was all about.

"Only the peasants can truly implement the revolutionary line of Chairman Mao," rationalized Chen Su-ching's production brigade primary schoolmaster, forty-year-old Huang Huo-chuan.

Accordingly, in each production brigade, the peasants elected a representative from their ranks to a committee of officials and educators that set school policy. The peasant delegate regularly visited the school to handle payments and administrative details and to assess material needs. This responsibility often bore practical fruit: If the school requested more desks and chairs, the peasants could cut the timber and build the furniture themselves.

The advisory committee recommended the content of textbooks. The peasant members usually suggested lessons that set examples, such as the song about the soldier defending his country.

Peasants also taught some primary and junior middle school classes. These peasant teachers were usually junior middle school graduates themselves. After they had accumulated experience in the rice fields, they were assigned to the school by their production teams, which continued to pay them on the basis of work-points. They conducted classes alongside the professional teachers assigned to the commune by the government. The government teachers were salaried and received higher wages than their peasant colleagues; schoolmaster Huang admitted he earned $36 a month (excluding food grain)—"the maximum monthly salary," he said.

Both groups of teachers, who participated in identical class assignments, refreshed their preparation in several weekly political seminars and study sessions.

The peasants also helped implement a new part-work, part-study program. Under the direction of local peasants, school children like Chen Su-ching went to the rice fields and factories to learn how those agricultural and industrial concepts they studied in class were put into practice.

"Before the Cultural Revolution," recalled brigade teacher Huang, "due to Liu Shao-chi's revisionist line, our teaching was theoretical. These children didn't know the difference between a stalk of rice and a peanut plant.

"But now, with the leadership of the poor and lower-middle peasants, we take study out of the classroom into the countryside."

The production brigade school cultivated its own small farm plot. Since the purpose of the farm was to instruct, the school administration was not concerned with earning a profit. But in 1972 the schoolmaster claimed, the school earned about $150 from the sale of rice and other crops, and the money helped pay for some school purchases such as sporting goods and farm implements.

Younger children like Chen Su-ching spent only one hour a week on the school's small farm or in a commune factory, accompanied by their teachers. They were also responsible for cleaning their classrooms.

Older students dedicated several hours a week to physical labor, often tilling the production team rice fields. They also spent two or three days a month observing skilled workers in local factories.

Farm work at the senior middle school was also included in the educational program. This school had two farm plots totalling about two and one-half acres, where each student was required to work a minimum of one-half day a week. Like their younger comrades in the villages, the senior middle school students used the crop sales to pay school expenses; they also consumed some of their home-grown harvest in the school canteen.

Theoretically, senior middle school was the stepping-stone to a university, but there was little chance of advancement for Kwang Li's students. Since the Cultural Revolution, senior middle school students graduated exclusively to full-time work in the fields. Enrollment at China's universities was severely restricted, and those who wished to attend were required to spend at least two years in the fields or in a factory. This program was known as "re-educated youth," "sent-down youth," or "youth to the countryside."

The object was to avoid the dilemma of some other Asian nations, with a surplus of over-educated scholars and scientists, too sophisticated to relate to the basic challenges of rural poverty.

In theory, the re-educated-youth program was a stepping-stone to higher education, but the cruel reality for most of China's intellectual, aspiring youth was that they would never be selected to attend a university because there was no room—and, in the CCP view, no urgent national priority for the sophisticated curriculum the university taught.

It hardly seemed necessary for indigenous commune youth to go to the fields to acquire practical knowledge of peasant life; yet they were required to participate in the program along with city-dwellers who had never seen a paddy field.

Even if the middle school graduates complied with the requirements, their prospects for higher education were not bright: With characteristic Chinese impassivity, senior middle schoolmaster Hsu admitted that thus far not one of his school's graduates had been accepted for a university course in the five years the school had been in operation.

By the time we talked with the emigrant from Kwang Li, who was himself a "re-educated youth" from Canton, he said as far as he knew, one local Kwang Li youth had matriculated to the university in 1972 and two others had followed in 1973. They may not have been senior middle school graduates, since senior middle school was not a prerequi-

A senior middle school student tills the school plot.

site for university admission, as practical labor was. Possibly headmaster Hsu did not mention these individuals because they had attended senior middle school elsewhere, prior to 1968.

The odds against university admission probably did not seem too awesome for the sons and daughters of Kwang Li's farmers and factory workers; and the refugee in Hong Kong recalled that commune parents often felt it was not necessary to have too much schooling, since their children would end up farming. But the expectation of never entering a university appeared more worrisome to the young people from the cities who were serving their apprenticeship as "re-educated youth" at Kwang Li. Some three hundred fifty of these urban youth were working alongside Kwang Li's peasants in 1973; and by the summer of 1974, the emigrant in Hong Kong said the group had increased to about seven hundred persons.

These young men and women were locked into their fate: If they wanted to pursue further education, they had no choice but to go to the countryside, work hard, and hope to be chosen for the universities, though the call might never come.

In fact, the urban youth's chances of attending a university did not seem any greater than those of Kwang Li's own young people. The emigrant in Hong Kong said the same number (three) of the urban "re-educated youth" as Kwang Li's natives had been admitted to a university. A production team leader in Kwang Li also said that none of his "re-educated" protégés had been "asked" to return to school, under a quota system that appeared to determine selection.

The re-education program was not only intended to compel urban youth to confront the reality of rural China. According to a peasant team leader who supervised a group of these young people at Kwang Li, by initiating the city youth into the hardships of farm labor, the peasants were showing them how to be "real Communists." One could not help thinking the program was a potential source of trouble, if the young people became embittered by the prospect of a life of field labor.

No one among the peasants was particularly surprised, said the emigrant from Kwang Li, that he and his "re-educated" comrades were discontented with commune life. Even after he twice failed to leave the commune and flee to Hong Kong, he said the peasants did not treat him too badly when he was sent back to Kwang Li. He claimed escape attempts were common among "re-educated youth." However, if a peasant had tried to escape to Hong Kong, he said, the penalties were harsh and might include the public humiliation of a "struggle meeting."

K'u Chien-chien was a bright-eyed twenty-one-year-old "re-educated youth" who arrived in Kwang Li in December 1968 to answer Chairman Mao's call. At that time, seven other young people joined K'u in his production team. Subsequently three had left: one to join the People's Liberation Army and two to work in a factory. Another was teaching school under the peasant instructor program but still belonged to the original production team. So far, none of them had matriculated at a university.

A "re-educated youth" like K'u could request to continue his education, but first, according to K'u's production team leader, the peasants had to review the youth's performance to certify that he or she was "closely linked with the broad masses" and "thought wholeheartedly of serving the people."

Smoking a home-grown cigarette from his private plot, K'u Chien-chien discussed his chances for further education.

"I have never estimated how long I might have to wait," said this young man, opening and closing his calloused fingers. "As a revolutionary youth, I will wait as long as it takes." He spoke with a hint of resignation.

His wait had already lasted five years. During that time, K'u, whose father was a pharmacist and whose mother was a physician, had toiled like an ordinary peasant. He lived with two other city émigrés in a one-story brick hut in one of the commune's larger villages. Next to his threadbare grey pillow, he kept a flashlight. A small shotgun hung on a nail on the wall; he said he used it to hunt birds. (Chinese peasants were encouraged to eliminate scavengers.)

Predictably, K'u asserted that his experience had been positive.

"After several years here," he said, "I came to see that only through working with the peasants could I understand their qualities." Now, he reported, he had grasped the "consciousness of the collective."

"Only through this method," he said dogmatically, "can the restoration of capitalism be avoided."

K'u rationalized his own situation: He insisted that he did not miss his former life in the city—not even his parents, whom he saw about once a month.

"Here," he said, as if trying to convince himself, "we've been accepted by the poor peasants; and they're as good as our parents."

But perhaps this intense young man had not completely persuaded himself that he could happily spend his entire life in the rice fields. At one point, there was a slip of the tongue: Instead of talking about *"If I go on to the university,"* K'u distinctly said, *"When . . ."*

It was infinitely more difficult to penetrate the well-scrubbed facade of K'u's neighbor, twenty-three-year-old Lin Hsiao-mei. Lin, a graduate of a senior middle school in Canton, joined the re-education program along with K'u in 1968. She shared a partitioned brick room in K'u's dormitory with a thirteen-year-old commune girl whom she was teaching to read. The room contained two hard bunk beds, a mirror, and a dressing table. On the bureau top, preserved under glass, were several frayed, faded postcard-sized photographs of small groups of people standing awkwardly in a grassy park. These, Lin identified in halting English as her brothers, her sister, and schoolmates. A copy of Chairman Mao's red book of quotations lay on the dresser.

Although Lin had spent the first four years of her stay at Kwang Li toiling in the rice fields, spreading nightsoil (manure), and hardening her hands pulling weeds, she still looked more like a city dweller than a peasant. Unlike the peasants, she wore wire-rimmed spectacles that sparkled against the pale patina of her freckled face. She had a high forehead and an alert expression, which she accentuated by austerely pulling her hair into thick braids. Constantly animated, she beamed broadly when talking.

Lin Hsiao-mei's explanation of how she graduated from the rice fields to teach first grade in May 1972 became a point of pivotal ideological significance as we talked.

"I wanted to be a teacher," asserted Lin, waving a paper fan against the humid air. She admitted that as far back as 1966 and 1967 she had dreamed of teaching. As a senior middle school graduate, she had the basic qualifications for teaching, but when she became a "re-educated youth," she had to convey this idea to the peasants. They, she asserted, would decide if she should actually abandon the fields for the classroom. Here was her crucial dilemma: How would the peasants learn of her desire?

Lin insisted that she never formally requested to become a teacher.

"I never spoke to the representative of the poor peasants who is responsible for education," she told us. She stuck to the supposition that she was chosen for the job. Finally she conceded that she had told some of the peasants that she wanted to be a teacher. They duly conveyed the message to the leadership of the production team, so that she never burdened them with her direct request. It seemed she was playing the "re-educated youth" game to the hilt.

Even as she contemplated her future, Lin's goals were couched in CCP rhetoric. In response to a suggestion that further education might make her a better teacher, she replied as if that alternative had never occurred to her.

"Practical experience makes you a good teacher," she declared. "I'm not experienced, but now I'm learning. And besides, I only teach first grade." Lin's explanation conformed neatly to the CCP line that practical knowledge was an equitable substitute for institutional education.

Without blinking an eye, Lin said that if necessary she would return to farm labor without remorse. But under persistent interrogation, she finally admitted that "there is value in *wanting* to be a teacher."

Lin faithfully spouted the requisite CCP phrases about dedication to peasant life; but to see how well she had really adapted to country life, we asked city-bred Lin about the hefty rat that scuttled across the top of her kitchen shelf while we chatted. Was she afraid?

"Yes," she said, laughing openly for the first time and hunching her shoulders in a mock shudder. "I am afraid of rats."

The countryside had required some adjustments.

Should they ever enter a university, K'u, Lin and their "re-educated" classmates would probably bring a perspective more in tune with the realities of their society. But by scattering its young talent throughout the vast areas of China, the Peking leadership may also have created a potentially volatile situation. For as the young, educated class grew older and their expectations of returning to the city became more remote, their energy could galvanize as frustration and possibly as dangerous ferment.

15
MEDICAL CARE

In the austere operating room of Kwang Li's one-story hospital, a fifty-three-year-old peasant woman sat erect on the operating table. Moments before, a surgeon had successfully removed an egg-sized tumor from her throat. The commune surgeon gave her a fatherly tap on the shoulder, when unexpectedly, she piped up:

"Mao Chu-hsi wan sui!" She repeated the phrase three times, in a forced, thin voice.

" 'Long live Chairman Mao' !" translated our guide, smiling.

Then, with two nurses to steady her, the patient walked from the operating room under her own power.

Medical care was the most impressive feature we found on the commune. Rural medicine at Kwang Li revolved around a forty-four-bed commune hospital, a series of long, white-washed buildings in Kwang Li town. Along with its schools, the hospital was the pride of the commune. Rural hospitals are an extreme rarity in Southeast Asia. So every visitor to Kwang Li was ushered into the hospital for at least a quick look.

At the hospital, twenty-four doctors, each of whom had usually undergone a maximum of four years of university training, were assisted by twenty-four nurses.

Kwang Li hospital was a showplace. It had its own X-ray machine, installed in 1972, and an operating room. But most of the activity centered around an outpatient clinic—half a dozen examining rooms adjacent to the main entry. Its administrator said the hospital handled as many as three thousand outpatients every week, with the peak periods in the growing seasons. In the rear, flanking a small courtyard, were two convalescence wards. One was a large open room with about two dozen beds; the other building was divided into several smaller rooms.

These rooms were screened and airy, with clay-tiled floors, but otherwise they were unadorned.

By urban standards the hospital seemed primitive, but to the Chinese it signified a marked improvement in rural medical care; and the buildings, which reflected the rudimentary construction on the commune, were clean and well-kept.

Besides the hospital, each production brigade operated its own clinic, and a corps of village paramedics crisscrossed the commune periodically.

Commune medical care was not free, but the cost was low, and services were available to all—a situation unprecedented in the peasant villages of Asia. The hospital administrator said that the peasants paid their production brigades a monthly medical fee amounting to about 60 cents a year. There was a 10-cent charge for each visit to the hospital and a 5-cent fee at the village clinics. First the peasants paid for medication; later the production brigade reimbursed them.

Dr. Kwok Ho-kuang, Kwang Li's thirty-two-year-old surgeon, said that most local diseases were seasonal. However, the most common ailment was indigestion. Most other problems—bronchitis, pneumonia, and coughs—occurred in the cold, wet winter months. Influenza caused the most serious epidemics, the doctor reported, noting the progress since pre-1949 times when tuberculosis and childbed (puerperal) fever took a heavy toll of lives in this area.

"We believe in prevention first, curing second," said Dr. Kwok. He said that each peasant underwent a general physical examination every year, and that the commune followed a prescribed regimen for inoculations, including diphtheria, polio, smallpox, cholera, and tetanus shots.

"We have not had a case of very serious infectious disease such as smallpox and cholera in Kwang Li for the past fifteen years," Dr. Kwok added affirmatively. (In China we also saw fewer afflictions such as scalp tumors, goiter, and the grotesque skin infections that are common in the Far East, where simple remedies are often beyond the means of many people.)

Hospital employees supervised a widespread public health program. Under normal circumstances, each production brigade designated certain members to promote cleanliness. The hospital administrator said that whenever necessary the hospital would also dispatch sanitation workers to the villages. Through a hospital health education program, messages were broadcast over the commune radio station and dis-

Dr. Kwok Ho-Kuang, surgeon.

Below: *Huang Ho-fu, "barefoot doctor," one of Kwang Li's paramedics.*

tributed on billboards, explaining procedures for cleaning houses and preventing disease, and admonishing the peasants to wash certain vegetables and boil drinking water. Staff members also inspected food prepared by local shops and restaurants.

Dr. Kwok told us that schistosomiasis (an endemic disease caused by a parasitic worm passed in human feces) had not previously been the problem in the Kwang Li region it had in other areas of China. Nevertheless, the commune only used feces as fertilizer after they were soaked with germicides in three stages and then fermented to kill the bacteria and possible worm eggs.

The hospital operated two pharmacies. One dispensed Western medicines; the other administered Chinese drugs such as medicinal herbs. The Chinese pharmacy was a recent innovation inspired by a suggestion from Chairman Mao during the Cultural Revolution. The efficacy of Chinese potions had been a bone of medical controversy until, in a 1965 message now canonized as the June 26th Directive, Mao instructed the country to emphasize medical care in the rural areas. This recommendation led to a revival of traditional Chinese medicine: the application of herbs and the use of acupuncture. Chinese authorities were thus able to expand the scope of medical care.

In Kwang Li the directive prompted the opening of a Chinese pharmacy, and the hospital recruited several doctors, including an acupuncturist, to practice traditional Chinese medicine. A cursory examination of these techniques indicated that this medicine included some elements of homeopathy and that many of the herbs and roots prescribed were the raw materials from which certain Western medicines are derived.

The experience of Dr. Kwok Ho-kuang revealed how deeply the June 26th Directive had penetrated. Dr. Kwok, a slight man with a pensive expression, had completed a six-year course at Chungsan Medical College in Canton, where he studied four years of Western medicine and one year of Chinese medicine before serving one year's internship.

Dr. Kwok, a native of a nearby rural area, was the son of a waiter and a sales clerk; both were retired. Though his own family were not farmers, Dr. Kwok observed that in recent years the sons and daughters of peasants found it easier to enter medicine.

Of all medical graduates after 1965, about 70 percent were the children of peasants, he told us, indicating another result of Chairman Mao's emphasis on rural medicine and self-sufficiency.

"When I graduated, there was a shortage of doctors in the countryside, so the party issued a call to serve the peasants," said the doctor earnestly. "I responded and requested to work in the countryside."

The bright-eyed Dr. Kwok said he earned $29 a month. He lived on the hospital grounds with his wife, who was employed as a pharmacist at $28.50 monthly.

Dr. Kwok told us that, like any other salaried official on the commune, he was supposed to take his turn working with the peasants in the fields. Those words provoked an alarming image: How could a highly trained surgeon harden his sensitive hands scattering fertilizer? But Dr. Kwok dispelled our concern, explaining that this system merely established an easy way for the peasants to see the doctors and a good opportunity to spend their time in the fields teaching the "barefoot doctors" (the commune paramedics).

In contrast to Dr. Kwok's more institutionalized academic career, Dr. Su Tien-ao, a twenty-nine-year-old acupuncturist, served an apprenticeship to learn his trade. Dr. Su said he acquired his skills in the Kwang Li hospital, working under the tutelage of an elderly practitioner of Chinese medical science. Dr. Su learned acupuncture through the most practical of methods: He tried the needle many times on his own body.

Dr. Su exuded a surprising aura of self-assurance, considering how little the medical community understood the physiological mechanisms of acupuncture. Later we had an opportunity to witness a memorable incident when his confidence was tested dramatically.

Since the Bamboo Curtain lifted for American journalists in 1971, probably no single aspect of life in China had stimulated more interest than acupuncture. It was a subject of worldwide fascination that had reached cult proportions. Nonetheless, we were surprised to find that the use of acupuncture as an anesthetic had become so widespread throughout China that it was being used in rural hospitals. At Kwang Li, we were told, doctors had been using acupuncture anesthesia since January 1973. We were invited to witness the seventh operation performed locally using this technique.

9:00 A.M.: The patient was a fifty-three-year-old peasant woman exhibiting the gaunt physique of a hyperthyroid. Her tumor bulged along the right side of her throat. Nurses strapped her on the operating table and Dr. Su, the acupuncturist, chatted pleasantly with her as he prepared her right wrist.

The operating theater was a small whitewashed room with a white tile floor. It was distinguished by being the only room we encountered at Kwang Li that was not decorated with a portrait of Chairman Mao.

9:10: The acupuncturist inserted two long, fine needles into the patient's right wrist. She reported no discomfort.

9:15: Dr. Kwok, the surgeon, swabbed the patient's neck with an orange antiseptic. Meanwhile the acupuncturist rotated the acupuncture needles, inserted between the thumb and index finger of her hand. She said her right arm was becoming numb.

When one of the lamps flickered, someone jiggled and repositioned the plug, and we were reminded that the technical facilities here were primitive.

9:20: There were three nurses. One of them blocked off a working area on the patient's throat with sterile sheets. The patient's head was partially covered, so she could not see her neck.

When the patient reported complete numbness in her right arm and along her neck, Dr. Su stopped rotating the acupuncture needles. He then connected the needles to a small plastic console powered by four "D"-cell flashlight batteries, which generated enough current to induce a slight tremor in the woman's wrist. This had the same effect as manually rotating the needles.

The patient said she had lost feeling along her neck, so the operation began.

9:30: As the acupuncturist looked on, the surgeon, assisted by the three nurses, made a simple lateral incision bisecting the egg-sized tumor, which commune doctors had already determined was not malignant. As he cut the tissue away from the tumor, the surgeon checked with the patient, who still said she felt no pain. Her face was visible under the sheets, and she exhibited no discomfort.

10:00: The surgeon removed the tumor. Apparently unaware of this, the patient inquired how much longer the operation would last. Her arm was numb, and she said it bothered her.

10:07: A moment of drama! The operation was proceeding without complication, and the surgeon was working to close the incision, when the acupuncturist inadvertently jarred his acupuncture console. Simultaneously the patient's hand flopped over and lay immobile, the palm resting upward.

The tremor had ceased! A look of consternation passed across the acupuncturist's face. His first remedy was to tap the console, first

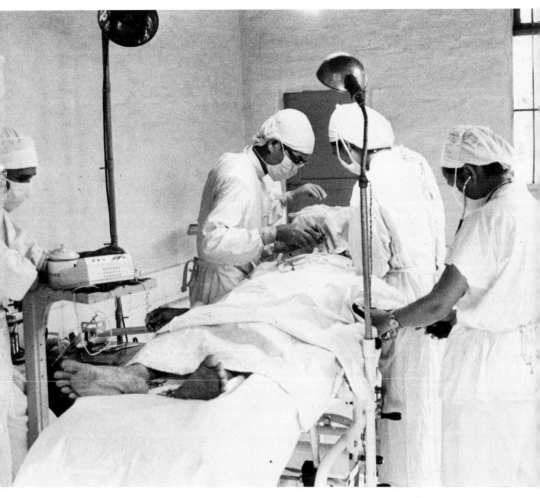

Acupuncture enabled the surgeon to talk with the patient throughout the operation.

lightly, then more vigorously. But the woman's wrist lay limp.

The surgeon meantime was unaware of the dilemma and proceeded to close the incision.

What thoughts passed through the mind of the acupuncturist at this point were unrecorded. Quickly he unscrewed the back of the console, removed the batteries, and realigned them.

Mercifully, the tremor resumed.

During the few moments the acupuncture device ceased functioning, the patient gave no indication she was feeling any pain. However, since her face was curtained off from the incision, the patient could not see what went wrong.

10:12: The patient complained that her pillow was too low, so the nurse adjusted it.

10:25: When the operation was over, the patient walked from the operating room under her own power, minus one thyroid tumor and apparently no worse for the wear.

The fee for this operation was $6. The peasant woman would pay it, receive a receipt, and, according to Dr. Kwok, be reimbursed from her production brigade's coffers. This operation formerly cost $15, but Dr. Kwok pointed out that after replacing traditional anesthetic medication with acupuncture, the hospital reduced the charge.

On a narrow village path, a solemn-faced man strutted briskly toward a brick house. Slung over his shoulder was a satchel with a red cross, which identified him as a "barefoot doctor," one of Kwang Li's paramedics. Huang Ho-fu was beginning a house call.

Inside the house, Huang sat at a dining table beside his patient, who complained of indigestion. He took her temperature and her pulse, measured her blood pressure, and peered into her throat. He asked for symptoms, then wrote a prescription in English. He shook out a few capsules from the bottles he kept in his silk-lined kit and carefully wrapped the pills in small squares of paper. He told the woman how to use the medicine, then packed up his gear and proceeded on his rounds.

Huang Ho-fu, twenty-three, whose expression was characterized by bold determination, was one of 108 barefoot doctors who treated the forty-three thousand residents of Kwang Li. Assisted by ten midwives, Huang and four other paramedics (one of them a woman) cared for the twenty-three hundred members of his production brigade.

The barefoot doctors did not have any illusions about the sophistication of their medical knowledge. Huang said he referred all serious cases to the commune hospital. When confronted with a serious accident, he said he applied emergency measures; and he called for the commune jeep to transport urgent cases. But like most barefoot doctors, Huang would treat common ailments: colds, coughs, sore throats, indigestion, slight fevers. He also felt qualified to treat minor accidents and apply stitches.

"Most illnesses in the countryside are common diseases," Huang explained. "Before we had barefoot doctors, if a peasant caught cold, he would have to go all the way to the hospital. This wasted time and prevented him from working in the fields. Now we treat these cases in ten minutes."

Huang began his training in 1967, when he spent four months in a barefoot doctors' class at the commune hospital. Subsequently he participated in a two months' refresher course. (The hospital held such supplementary courses every two years.) Huang said he learned more about medicine whenever doctors from the commune or county hospitals visited his village.

Like everyone else, the barefoot doctors were expected to do their share of agricultural work. Huang said he spent about one-third of his time toiling in the fields, and he was paid field-worker wages. He carried his medical kit with him and treated patients who worked alongside him.

Huang said he chose a medical career when he learned of the shortage of doctors in the countryside. He wanted to help peasants like his family who suffered from disease "before Liberation." But his horizons were limited. He claimed he had no interest in becoming a physician.

"If someone can go to medical school, that's fine," he said, frowning intently, "but China does not have many medical schools. So we do things our own way. With additional training and work, we barefoot doctors can raise our standards."

His outlook was typical of young people in China who were given large responsibilities with relatively little training. Rather than lament their lack of formal education, they were fiercely determined to learn on the job and do their best.

16
THE CHINESE COMMUNIST PARTY

Throughout China, blazoned across whitewashed walls and stone fences, doorposts and lintels, stentorian red Chinese characters trumpeted the slogans of China's new ideology.

"Serve the people!" declared the five most familiar Chinese characters, painted on countless walls and signboards, since this CCP slogan was used to inspire almost every civic action.

By its own definition, the Chinese Communist Party directed the moral leadership of Kwang Li—a weighty responsibility even in simplest terms. In reality, the CCP was also the real power behind the Revolutionary Committee's civilian, secular throne.

The CCP reached into all phases of commune life. Each neighborhood production team had a party group of at least three persons, and there was a CCP branch office in each village production brigade.

At the commune administration level, a separate CCP committee of seventeen persons, mostly composed of production brigade leaders or other officials, reviewed operations in the commune and saw whether CCP policy was being implemented. At Kwang Li, there were no specially designated poor-peasant representatives on the list at the time of our visit.

Though many commune residents might aspire to CCP membership, the road to acceptance into this all-powerful group was limited to those who adhered to official doctrine.

Someone who wished to join the party had to follow a complex procedure. The vice-chairman of the commune's administrative committee, Liang Wei-ming, named five major steps.

First, a prospective Communist must "strive hard to study Mao Tse-tung thought and Marxism-Leninism"—the core of commune ide-

"The four seas are rising, clouds and waters raging/The five continents are rocking, wind and thunder roaring!" Chairman Mao's verses framed the entrance to commune headquarters.

ology. Second, the applicant should "serve the people the world over wholeheartedly." Third, the candidate was admonished to combine the criticism of others with self-criticism and be willing to acknowledge and remedy his or her own deviations from the CCP line. Fourth, said Liang, constantly spouting textbook polemics, the applicant must "unite all the forces which can be united." Finally, when the candidate was trained in "the practical experience of working with the masses," Liang said he or she would submit an essay-form application expressing valid reasons for wishing to join the CCP. Then, two CCP members would write references and introduce the petitioner to the local CCP branch. Subsequently, local members would decide if the applicant qualified for membership.

Through all this, Vice-Chairman Liang sounded as if he were reciting Scripture; but often his liturgy made practical sense against the backdrop of Kwang Li, where leadership opportunities were limited, and where unity of thought and purpose had proved effective in remolding a primitive society.

Enough Kwang Li residents had passed through this screening process to increase the ranks of local CCP membership from over five hundred persons in 1963 to more than eight hundred a decade later. (Top officials were vague about the exact number on their roster.) In a commune with a population of roughly forty-three thousand, the CCP was therefore a statistical elite. Presumably Peking recognized the danger of elitism, and this partially explained the motivation for the Cultural Revolution, which attempted to integrate CCP members more fully among the peasants and workers.

CCP members exercised some voice in selecting their leaders, but this process was no more democratic than the elections for the Revolutionary Committee. Every two years, the county CCP organ submitted a list of names for approval by a local congress of commune CCP members.

The local CCP committee consisted of only seventeen members, whereas the Revolutionary (administrative) Committee had thirty-four (with the seventeen additional slots filled by government service cadres).

In 1968, when the county CCP officials were seeking a leader for Kwang Li's new Revolutionary Committee, they chose someone who was not born and raised on this commune. By recruiting forty-one-year-old Liang Nien from outside the commune, they demonstrated an ancient Chinese practice that was utilized during the Cultural Revolution: importing nonindigenous personnel into rural settings to impose uniform order. These officials were directly responsible to Peking rather than to a local power base. Besides, Liang Nien was a veteran of the People's Liberation Army (PLA), which played a major role in the Cultural Revolution.

The chairman of Kwang Li's Revolutionary and CCP committees had the ruddy cheeks and the aging, paunchy physique of an Irish politician, but with Liang Nien, irony replaced Irish-type wit. When Liang traveled through the commune raising his hand in lofty acknowledgment, the peasants greeted him with well-programmed hand waving.

Liang Nien, who said he was "prepared to be assigned anywhere," had worked his way up the administrative ladder, rung by rung. After fighting for the Communists during the Civil War, the young Liang became an army clerk. Liang then held administrative posts in Kao Yao county, in which Kwang Li was located. He said he first visited Kwang Li while serving on a postwar work team. (After the Communist takeover, work teams prepared the peasants for the changes in their way of life under the new system.) Subsequently Liang supervised the land redistribution of the early 1950s, and later the inspection of county-wide water conservation and insecticide projects. In 1965 he was appointed secretary of the CCP committee of another people's commune; in 1968 the county Revolutionary Committee selected him for the number one administrative post at Kwang Li.

After his transfer to Kwang Li, the people of the commune went through a quasi-democratic ritual of approving his appointment.

Liang Nien and Vice-Secretary Liang Wei-ming talked of their special responsibilities to instruct the people about politics, especially the teachings of Chairman Mao. CCP leaders at Kwang Li were charged with explaining the complicated rhetorical literature that spouted from Peking. This incessant flow of CCP line, with its obscure references, often seemed like little more than gibberish to the peasants, until local leaders interpreted these proclamations into concepts the people could comprehend.

It was easy to see how deviations developed, with seventy-five thousand communes interpreting Peking.

Liang Nien explained that the people of Kwang Li needed continuous, repeated political instruction, because even though they were well aware of the evils of capitalism, the struggle against "capitalistic tendencies" in the Chinese countryside had not ended.

Speaking metaphorically, Liang went on: "There are two roads, the socialist road and the capitalist road, which persons in the Chinese countryside can take. Our fundamental political education is concerned with this choice.

"During the Proletarian Cultural Revolution," Liang said, echoing CCP doctrine word for word, "the targets of our criticism were only those persons in authority taking the capitalist road.

"In the beginning, many people [peasants] didn't understand this, but they learned," he added.

It was hard to imagine any real or potential political initiative at Kwang Li that could have the slightest chance of undermining the commune system. But the party functionaries had been instructed not to be complacent.

In order to further disseminate the CCP credo, Liang and his colleagues organized political meetings and broadcast Peking's interpretation of the news on more than ten thousand loudspeakers connected to every house and public building.

Congenial, exuberant Vice-Chairman Liang Wei-ming portrayed Kwang Li's political education program as though it were a form of entertainment. Yet this was the mass indoctrination that had given China its image of enforced thought.

Liang Nien, Liang Wei-ming, and other Kwang Li officials insisted that "correct" political thinking could influence every aspect of life. In fact, Kwang Li's vice-chairman predicted that political awareness could even increase agricultural production. However when Liang Wei-ming acknowledged such nagging problems as the need for more tractors, his mood grew pensive. There was an underlying realization that the CCP still had to support its unceasing stream of maxims and proverbs with palpable evidence of material success.

Liang Wei-ming tempered his evaluation.

"China's development has just begun," he reminded his listeners.

17

POLITICS: A WAY OF LIFE

"I am a little member of the people's commune," sang a high-treble chorus of gaily dressed tots in Kwang Li's kindergarten, as their teacher pumped out the accompaniment on a small organ. Obeying what appeared to be a class rule, they sat with their hands behind their backs, so only their heads and shoulders would sway to the melody.

"After school, I go home," they warbled, slightly off-key. "I help my peasant uncles cut and harvest the rice.

"The peasants are exemplary people. We must learn from them." Their tiny heads bobbed in dutiful assent.

The words were harmless, but it was no coincidence that they stressed one of the main themes of the Cultural Revolution. As the vanguard of revolution, the peasants would lead the way to the future progress of all China. On the commune, political indoctrination began at a tender age.

Politics was as much a part of the peasants' daily fare as their rice. The CCP didn't want the peasantry to falter for a moment in their assimilation of party dogma, so the commune leaders disseminated Peking's message through a variety of methods. Often local CCP leaders like Liang Wei-ming relied on mass rallies to communicate official doctrine. Requiring the cadres to work directly among the peasantry in the fields also served this purpose. And within the production brigades and production teams, CCP members supervised the party's proselytizing on the most fundamental peasant-to-peasant basis.

Study meetings were the grass-roots political experience in rural China. In production teams, groups of twenty to thirty peasants participated in study meetings at regular intervals. To make the study meetings schedule easier for everyone to remember, the people of one Kwang Li production team congregated after sundown every fifth night, following market day.

One night, after a production team leader sounded a police whistle, we watched as peasants from a study group gathered outside a village house. The audience listened intently as a "re-educated youth" read from an official text. Then they were encouraged to offer personal comments. Usually they responded with party quotations. The elderly related how their present prosperity contrasted with their pre-Communist poverty. (These "speak-bitterness" recollections of pre-Liberation days had been a major feature of rural politics since the CCP first came to the Kwangtung countryside. We pondered what the CCP would do when the generation of older peasants who lived in the countryside before 1949 had passed away and could no longer describe the first-hand experience of their former hardships, thus highlighting the achievements of Communism.)

K'u Chien-chien, one of the "re-educated youths" who tilled the soil in Sui Kang production brigade, regularly conducted study meetings and occasionally attended commune-wide meetings for group leaders.

With the CCP insisting that only the peasants possessed real appreciation of the challenges confronting China, it seemed mildly ironic that a city youth was leading the country farmers in their political lessons. But K'u assured us that he was qualified to conduct the meetings, by virtue of his ability to read difficult phrases, a skill many of the peasants did not possess, and because his education had taught him how to relate CCP doctrine to agricultural production.

Since the crops were just reaching maturity, K'u read to his study group from a *People's Daily* article entitled "We must have a very great enthusiasm in developing agriculture." About two dozen peasants, gathered in a semicircle around K'u, leaned forward, listening intently.

"After the Cultural Revolution and the campaign of criticism and rectification," K'u recited, fanning himself with his text when he paused, "the people's commune collective economy has strengthened; and production in various fields has greatly increased."

Such vague generalities hardly incite debate in a country with as uniform a system of political conduct as China. Accordingly, the peasants supplemented K'u's half-hour discourse by merely reinforcing the article's thesis.

"First, we have to work at agricultural production," said a middle-aged man whose tawny, muscular shoulders protruded starkly from his sleeveless undershirt.

"By employing Chairman Mao's thought, we can improve production," he said, his phrases clicking in rapid Cantonese.

A young woman with thick hair matted against her forehead hoisted a pouting infant on her knee and thrust herself upright to peer over the people seated in front of her. With a fretful glance at her squirming child, she chimed in that "to improve their lives, the peasants have to set difficult goals and strive for them."

An old man, whose stubbly gray hair dipped into a point above his face like the visor of a cap, stopped sucking a reed pipe to venture, "The present crop output isn't bad, but more hard work remains."

Essentially the peasants were sycophants, adding their voices to the CCP monologue. But this was how the CCP hoped to stimulate political awareness.

Though the peasants' participation in these meetings probably had some effect on their stature within the community, their attendance and input were not supposed to be reflected in their income.

"The peasants' attitudes toward meetings don't count toward their wages," a young farm worker insisted, "only whether they work diligently."

It was difficult to assess the importance of attendance at these meetings and even more risky to analyze their long-term impact. But study meetings were conducted with ritualistic regularity, and the turnout was predictably high.

The mass media offered another conduit for conveying ideology and information. From its studios in a cardboard-partitioned loft above a wine cellar in downtown Kwang Li, a wired-radio system bombarded the commune population with news and propaganda for two-hour periods, three times daily.

Beneath the gaze of a paperweight-sized bust of Chairman Mao, the station's three announcers took turns reading the news and educational items and playing recordings of martial music, opera, and drama. The studio even had a rudimentary control panel. The announcers tape-recorded all their remarks, inhibiting any controversial ad libs.

Initially the only receivers for the commune broadcasts were loudspeakers wired to production brigade headquarters. Then the commune encouraged the peasants to install speakers in their homes and in all public buildings, and the production brigade leaders inspected to see that the home speakers were functional. By the end of 1971, Liang Wei-ming said emphatically, every house had one. In fact, he reported

Commune radio: Peking-style information, martial music and opera.

gleefully, some homes had more than one speaker.

The speakers were inexpensive—only about 55 cents. At last count, Liang said the commune could broadcast through ninety-eight hundred home-receiver speakers and five hundred public loudspeakers. Even when they switched off their private systems, commune residents could hardly avoid the programs, which droned from speakers in all corners of the commune.

In addition, most production brigades operated their own broadcast facilities, and some families had shortwave radio receivers which picked up programs from the cities. (Hong Kong Chinese-language stations were jammed.)

There was no pretense of impartiality in the broadcasts. In the presence of American journalists, the local newsreader called on his listeners to "continue to support Vietnam, Cambodia, and Laos against the United States." In his commentary, the broadcaster hailed the "struggle of the people" in Asia, Latin America, and Africa and their opposition to the superpowers. He outlined the enlargement of the European Economic Community and commented on the world armament situation, Japan's new foreign policy, and the "worsened relationship" between Egypt and the Soviet Union—issues that could not possibly have meant much to the average Kwang Li peasant. Somewhat closer to home, he reiterated a plea to "continue Chairman Mao's revolutionary foreign policy and the policy of peaceful coexistence with all countries." He went on to remind his listeners of the visits to China of U.S. President Nixon and the Japanese Prime Minister Tanaka, as well as the establishment of diplomatic relations with some twenty countries in the past year. He noted that Peking still condemned former head of state Liu Shao-chi and the Soviet "deceit and military expansion," and he concluded his commentary by calling upon the people to "continue the revolution, not be too self-contented with past achievement, have self-awareness of one's weaknesses at all times, and continue to be with the masses."

The broadcast station served as more than an instrument of propaganda. Its announcer regularly informed the people of local, county, and national news and of agricultural and industrial developments. The station also issued daily weather forecasts from the commune's meteorological laboratory, a facility Liang Wei-ming described as "very simple."

Concomitantly, the party carried out an equally broad dissemination of practical advice. Commune officials erected blackboards at public gathering places all over the commune. One such blackboard newspaper, located outside the hospital, advised people to wash their vegetables and boil drinking water. Chalk illustrations for the benefit of illiterates accompanied each written message.

Publishing in China was under the control of the state. The commune administration operated a bookstore in Kwang Li town, something few villages in other Asian lands could boast of having. The shelves contained some technical tracts and a few literary texts, including numerous children's stories, which were also popular among elderly, semiliterate peasants. But the publications were unfailingly laced with the CCP message, and the major portion of the literature was unadulterated propaganda.

The bookshop also sold colorful posters, which decorated many peasant homes and buildings. Poster subjects included scenes from Chinese operas or movies, or such traditional themes as Chairman Mao in various stages of his youth, great moments of CCP history, and portraits of the approved pantheon: Chairman Mao, Marx, Engels, Lenin, and Stalin.

In addition, nearly four thousand copies of the local area CCP newspaper circulated on the commune.

The CCP also exploited the power of the arts to influence as well as to entertain. In traditional China, the arts were considered vehicles of moral instruction, and Chairman Mao stressed this would continue to be their function in the new society when he delivered his "Talks at the Yenan Forum on Literature and Art" in 1942.

Peasant exposure to the politicized arts and peasant creativity blossomed in recent years with the formation of rural propaganda teams. Kwang Li had a commune propaganda team of thirty to forty volunteers plus smaller teams in the production brigades. In their spare time, team members composed many skits and songs. They also performed selections from a national repertory of music, drama, and dance.

The commune dispatched small cultural teams into the mountains for brief performances. But the major thrust was directed towards gala propaganda shows in the larger villages.

Propaganda shows were the most elaborate and sophisticated means of spreading the CCP message in the countryside. These live extravaganzas very much resembled old-time medicine shows.

On one typical Saturday night, several thousand peasants squeezed into Sui Kang production brigade's stuffy, vault-shaped auditorium. Inside they waved bamboo fans as bats swooped overhead amid the wooden rafters.

This performance was a bit special. Only once each month a traveling propaganda team from the county would join the commune team, and this month the sophisticated county players were performing in Sui Kang village. Both teams were dressed in the colorful costumes of various professional, regional, and ethnic groups. They wore stage make-up and elaborate hair fashions. Their performance was enhanced by dramatic lighting and scenery on a stage framed with red velvet curtains.

At first, it was difficult to judge the peasant audience's reaction. They applauded respectfully to a few stilted instrumental versions of traditional folktunes given new titles, e.g., "Spring Comes Early When Men Work Diligently." Next, a chubby, rouged female vocalist in a baggy gray Mao suit squeaked out an off-key version of "I Love My Great Motherland" to the accompaniment of an accordion. But the peasants noticeably warmed to a song and dance interpretation of "Tachai Is Excellent." The performers, attired in the flowing striped caftan-style robes of the minority peoples in Sinkiang Province, bounded vigorously about the stage. The minority costumes were supposed to demonstrate national unity under communism. The lead vocalist flailed his arms expansively to indicate his enthusiasm for the ideological content of the lyrics, but his gestures also matched the joyous spirit of the rousing melody.

The high point of the evening came just before intermission. Adapting the traditional Cantonese opera style, three actors from the commune propaganda team portrayed the story of Kwang Li barefoot doctors who discovered an herb that supposedly relieved chronic bronchitis. These peasants gave a spirited performance in a skit they had composed and choreographed themselves and embellished with simple scenery representing trees and a thatched hut.

The protagonists in this short but significant moral drama were rural medical workers Dr. Chang and his assistant, Li Yu-ying, and an elderly woman patient, Chou. As the curtains squeaked open, the medical duo came onstage, singing of their duties to prevent and cure disease. They attributed their inspiration to Chairman Mao, who emphasized medical care in the rural areas.

"We must think of all means to cure old-age bronchitis," the young woman sang earnestly, "and contribute a share more to the revolution!"

"Right! Think of the people!" echoed the male lead.

Revolutionary altruism seemed incongruous when dramatized with the gesticulations and operatic bravado that once helped convey moral lessons such as filial piety in traditional Chinese theater. But today as always, the peasants responded to this exaggerated style, so it was an effective and painless way of sugar-coating Peking's message.

As the plot unfolded, the barefoot doctors disclosed that they were searching for herbs as a cure for bronchitis, when they stumbled upon a plant called *jia-diao-chung,* known to aid digestion and the appetite.

One of the tenets of the barefoot doctor program dictated that the medical workers should perform experiments upon themselves if necessary: therefore, they should taste this medicine. Fortunately, this herb was not poisonous!

After praising a local medical research team—even singing the statistics summarizing the team's findings—the peasant performers reiterated that they must continue to strive for future success.

The scene then shifted to the home of the patient, a peasant woman who informed the audience with thespian gusto that after suffering chronic bronchitis for twenty years and spending several hundred dollars in large hospitals, she was finally cured by inexpensive local herbs here in Kwang Li.

The miniature medical drama was assured of a happy ending because, she informed the barefoot doctors, she could now return to "productive labor."

Obviously this operatic skit represented more than just a pleasant diversion. While amusing the audience, it demonstrated that working for others could be a rewarding task, not just an obligation. The tale also praised the combination of Chinese and Western medicine and exalted the spirit of experimentation, themes which Peking strived to disseminate among the peasantry. The animated acting and convincing staging also revealed that peasant farmers could produce entertainment of a surprisingly professional standard.

By this time the audience was spellbound. The next item was also upbeat. To stage the "Dance of the Li People," the county propaganda team had brought elaborate moving props: cardboard cut-outs representing piles of grain, one of which was mounted on wheels. Again to stress harmonious relations with minority groups, the female dancers wore red dresses trimmed with yellow, the costume of an ethnic group from Hainan Island. The young girls carried cardboard, make-believe baskets in which, as a banner in the backdrop proudly proclaimed, they were donating their "patriotic grain" to the state. They swooped through the folk-dance as if they were propaganda posters come to life. In the final refrain, a male dancer costumed as a truck driver symbolically hauled the mobile pile of grain to the state granaries, assisted by stagehands who hid behind the cardboard cut-out "harvest" and pushed it offstage. The audience thundered its approval.

Subsequent skits were more static, but no less instructional. A young man and woman from Kwang Li performed a vocal duet, "Wish Chairman Mao Long Life," followed by solo selections, "I Love the Blue Ocean" and "The Great Peking." Next the commune propaganda team donned costumes of China's steppe peoples to sing a rousing chorus of "Red Guards of the Grasslands Have Seen Chairman Mao."

The evening ended with a complete scene from the revolutionary opera *Sha Chia Pang*. The female soloist wore a tunic over trousers and toddled on high block-like shoes. During the final scene, a major character "floated" onstage on board a cardboard boat.

Time after time, when the red velvet curtains closed on scenes that transported the captivated peasants far from their dusty rice culture into the realm of fantasy, it mattered little that the songs panegyrized Chairman Mao and the glories of revolution. This was entertainment, and the audience was enthralled.

For the peasants of Kwang Li People's Commune, life was still basically the same arduous, primitive struggle it had always been. Yet in many ways CCP rule touched these people in a positive fashion. By branding the peasants as heroes and exhorting the entire population to emulate them, Peking encouraged these humble farmers to be proud of their simple way of life. By directing all Chinese, from students to surgeons, to learn from the peasants, the CCP has set in motion forces intended to benefit the country-dwellers.

By elevating the plodding reliability of the peasantry to a national ideal, the CCP necessarily exalted the mundane. But in 1973, the peasants' collective efforts had produced a society that was comfortable and secure—an unprecedented achievement for China.

18
CONCLUSIONS

Chen Yung-tien was a hardy twenty-one-year-old who served in the commune militia. He had practiced firing a weapon, and, he insisted, as a member of the militia, it was his duty to "play a role in the vanguard of production to encourage the other peasants to work harder."

"Do you think there will ever be a war?" we asked.

The young man smiled, unable or unwilling to answer.

"We don't know," his father finally broke in. "There may be war, maybe not; but it is important to make preparations, in case of foreign invasions."

"Where does the danger come from?" we asked the young man.

"From the Soviet revisionists," Chen Yung-tien declared.

"What about the United States?" we asked, smiling.

Again the young man was stymied.

"We have many friends in America," his father chimed in.

The people of Kwang Li often paid lip service to ideals but conducted their lives along more pragmatic lines, as people of any culture might.

In their efforts to exhibit the "correct" ingestion of political teaching, many of the peasants learned to repeat verbatim the phrases disseminated by the CCP. But when they were asked to explain what the words meant, they were often incapable of articulating their meaning, and they revealed they might be mouthing platitudes that they did not really understand.

Yet the unquestioning acceptance of the CCP line reflected but another aspect of the continuity of life in rural China. Before the Chinese people memorized the thoughts of Chairman Mao, social scientists report that Chinese scholars used to recite the homilies of Confucius without really understanding their content.[7]

Unprecedented prosperity and security won more loyalty than political slogans.

In the countryside, we sensed that the abundance of food and the unprecedented security were much more politically persuasive than the continuing chorus of axioms from Chairman Mao.

Most of the residents of Kwang Li could recite CCP platitudes, but these maxims did not necessarily dictate how they lived.

Did the starch factory worker really contradict CCP ideals when, while buying a wrist watch for the utilitarian purpose of telling "what time to go to work," she decided among three models simply because one was prettier?

Was Lo Chin-loung really "serving the people" when she performed household chores so that her son and daughter-in-law could work in the fields? Or was she merely serving her family?

These were in fact pleasant discrepancies ("contradictions," to borrow the Maoist term), quirks, and idiosyncracies that made the commune a vibrant, humane society rather than a stale, cardboard replica of some utopian formula.

Other disparities between the spoken assertion and the actual situation were not so easy to accept. Commune women insisted they received equal pay for equal work; but when we examined the situation more intimately, we discovered they received less pay for different work. The commune surgeon explained how he "answered the call" to serve the rural people, when in reality he was assigned to his job. The "re-educated youths," said they volunteered to come to the countryside to learn from the peasants. They had no alternative; and they often ended up in the role of teachers conducting the peasants' political meetings.

But perhaps most distressing to us was the discrepancy between our preconceived image of rural China as an egalitarian society and the reality of a rural class structure which the CCP was perpetuating and exploiting. Rural leaders were still fanning the flames of jealousy and revenge, using the landlords and their offspring as scapegoats at least two decades after they had to relinquish their last claims to the land.

Bribery had disappeared, for all that we could observe at Kwang Li, but the CCP still tolerated the age-old Chinese practice of playing favorites. To us, all this seemed out of context in a society striving to eliminate elitism.

At the Saturday night propaganda show, we encountered an overt example of favoritism. In the dense crowd that packed into the production brigade auditorium, a front-of-the-house seat was a coveted item. The occupancy of this choice location was not left to chance. Tacked to the backs of the first twenty rows of wooden benches were squares of paper scrawled with numbers. There, in the reserved section, sat the "model families" from the production brigade, while a crowd of more humbly attired peasants had to struggle for admittance at the back of the hall. The doors were actually locked during the performance to keep the overflow away.

Throughout their lives, certain persons—beginning with the best students and the Little Red Soldiers—were singled out for preferential treatment. This attention was a reward for their exemplary behavior or, to repeat a favorite local phrase, "correct thinking." Special treatment could be a function of birth. The offspring of the poor and lower-middle peasants and cadres received priority. Inversely, the families of rich peasants and landlords, now in the second or third generation, were still suffering for the sins of their fathers.

When the CCP assumed power in 1949, China was in dire straits. Its people were suffering the effects of two devastating wars—the war with the Japanese and the civil war. The country was still splintered into thousands of communities without a common language, a system of transportation, or reliable means of communication.

The establishment of the people's communes in 1958 was loosely equivalent to drafting all the peasants into a people's army in order to mobilize the strength, will, and determination of the Chinese peasant community.

It was a drastic measure by all accounts, accompanied by suffering and failure, but in communities like Kwang Li, collectivization established a foundation for agricultural development that changed the course of history.

In a few decades, the residents of Kwang Li had created a community that compared favorably with rural peasant communities elsewhere in Asia. When contrasted with similar densely populated societies, life in the Chinese countryside was comfortable and the necessities were provided.

But the peasants of Kwang Li were in some ways trapped within the mass social experiment that had benefited them. People were not living in chains, but young peasants could not pick up stakes and leave. Only the government could offer jobs on the government's terms, and anyone who dreamed of a university education quickly learned how minimal the chances of admission were. Young Chinese peasants were required

"I am a people's soldier!" the ten-year-olds shouted.

to stay on the commune and work within the system or not at all.

Some of the young people learned the system well. Wo Mon-chun, a twenty-two-year-old pigtailed primary school teacher from Canton, cheerfully told us how she was assigned to teach music at the commune in 1968 under the program for "re-educated youth." We wondered if she were disappointed that she had not been selected to continue her education in a university.

Even before we could pose the question, Wo plunged on. "I will do what is best for my country. If the party needs me to stay here, I will spend the rest of my life here." Her cheeks glowed with enthusiasm.

Such idealism was disarming and perhaps misleading, but it was also refreshing. The people's constant references to a willingness to sacrifice for the common good were among our most uplifting impressions of Kwang Li. Whenever we asked about their ambitions, people said they wanted to "increase production" or "serve the people."

The people of Kwang Li were ambitious. If they played along with the system—and here that meant working together—there were personal rewards: more work-points or perhaps a chance to drive a tractor. Commune residents did not acknowledge their achievements as personal gain, but often they benefited personally, though many of them may sincerely have believed that they were simply dedicating their lives to the service of others. The CCP ideals offered an inspirational outlook on life's responsibilities and enshrined the mundane toil of Chinese country life with an aura of sanctity.

When the CCP took over in 1949, the peasants of Kwang Li were faced with the challenge of survival.

The ultimate victory over centuries of poverty belonged to the peasants. They did it with sweat, muscle, and a pioneering spirit, and their only resources were manpower and determination. Taken in that context, what happened at Kwang Li after 1949 appeared much more remarkable for what the peasants had gained, rather than for what they had lost.

Beaming like a rose-colored lantern, music teacher Wo Mon-chun led her class of primary students in song.

"I am a people's soldier," she sang in her brittle soprano.

"I am a people's soldier!" the classroom of ten-year-olds repeated, their lungs nearly bursting.

NOTES

1. C. K. Yang, "A Chinese Village in Early Communist Transition," in *Chinese Communist Society: The Family and the Village.* Fifth paperback printing. (Cambridge and London: The M.I.T. Press, 1972), p. 103.
2. Romanization of proper names at Kwang Li was provided by interpreters of the China International Travel Service.
3. This refugee (illegal emigrant in Chinese terminology, since "refugee" indicates flight, and that supposedly reflects poorly on the Chinese system) was twenty-two years old and a native of a small village on the edge of Canton (Kwangchow). In November 1968, he was sent down to work in the fields at Kwang Li People's Commune as part of the mass movement of city youth to the countryside during the Cultural Revolution. He had completed the first year of senior middle school; and in his youth he was a member of the Young Pioneers (the forerunner of the Little Red Soldiers). He said he had made three attempts to flee China. During the first two, he was apprehended, mildly chastised, and sent back to Kwang Li. On July 1, 1974, he swam to Hong Kong, where we interviewed him during the latter part of that month.
4. "A Visit to the Tungting People's Commune (III)—Its Three-level Ownership," *Peking Review,* No. 15 (April 13, 1973), p. 11.
5. C. K. Yang, interviewed with the authors on the *Marie Torre Show,* KDKA-TV, Pittsburgh, Pa., U.S.A., October 1, 1973.
6. The CCP viewed team-level ownership as a temporary measure to maintain harmony until such time as the people moved closer to a socialist ideal. Then ownership would revert to production brigade and people's commune levels and finally to the socialist state. Recent essays have conceded that this process would entail gradual development over considerable time. From "A Visit to the Tungting People's Commune (IV)—How a Production Team Carries on Its Work," *Peking Review,* No. 15 (April 20, 1973), p. 12.
7. John King Fairbank, *The United States and China,* third edition (Cambridge: Harvard University Press, 1971), pp. 69–70.

APPENDIX:
AGRICULTURAL STATISTICS*

Kwang Li People's Commune
Kao Yao County, Kwangtung Province, People's Republic of China

Land area: 258 square kilometers
   Land under cultivation: 9,500 acres
   Land under rice cultivation: 7,000 acres
   Timber land: 26,600 acres
   Irrigated land: 8,800 acres

Population: 43,000 (approx.)
   Households: 10,000 (approx.)

Rice production: (2 crops annually)
   Before 1949: 4.3 million *catties*
   1971:   45.76 million *catties*
   1972:   46.19 million *catties*
   1973:   50.50–51.00 million *catties* (projected)

Rice cultivation:
   1964: 800 *catties* per *mou*
   1966: 1100 *catties* per *mou*
   1971: 1182 *catties* per *mou*
   1972: 1193 *catties* per *mou*

*Chinese weights and measures used in this book:
                1 *mou* = ⅙ acre
                1 *catty* = ½ kilogram or 1.1 pounds
                1 *picul* = 100 catties, or 110 pounds
          1 Chinese foot = ⅓ meter
Chinese currency: 1 RMB = U.S. $0.50, at time this research was conducted

Rice reserves:
People's commune: 21,000 *catties*
Production brigades: 230,000 *catties*
Production teams: 1,160,000 *catties*
Private families: 1,600,000 *catties*

Rice taxes (1972) and state purchases:
State agricultural tax: 2,300,000 *catties*
Sales of surplus to state: 18,700,000 *catties*

Rice prices:
First grade rice: RMB 10.80 / 100 *catties*
                    (U.S. $4.90 / 100 pounds)
Second grade rice: RMB 10.30 / 100 *catties*
                    (U.S. $4.70 / 100 pounds)
Third grade rice: RMB 9.80 / 100 *catties*
                    (U.S. $4.45 / 100 pounds)

Rice consumption: (rationed to persons in town)
For heavy workers: 45 *catties* (50 pounds) / month
For ordinary workers: 36 *catties* (40 pounds) / month
For clerks: 30 *catties* (33 pounds) / month
For children: according to age

OTHER CROPS (Approximately 60 percent of land was devoted to second crops.)

Sugar cane:
1971: 16,000 tons
1972: 21,800 tons
1973: 25,000 tons (projected)

Peanuts:
1972: 830,000 *catties*
1973: 900,000–1,000,000 *catties* (projected)

Hemp:
1972: 110,000 *catties*
1973: 350,000 *catties* (projected)

Tangerines:
1972: 140,000 *catties*
1973: 170,000 *catties* (projected)

Other fruits (lychees, longans, pears, bananas, water chestnuts, lotus roots, etc.): 480,000 *catties* annually

Garlic:
1972: 1.2 million *catties*
1973: 1.5 million *catties* (projected)

Yams:
1972: 580,000 *catties*
1973: 650,000 *catties* (projected)
Candied yams: over 100,000 *catties* annually

Timber:
1971: 3,400 cubic meters
1972: 3,460 cubic meters
1973: 3,700 cubic meters (projected)

Resin:
1971: 1 million *catties*

Honey:
1971: 80,000 *catties*

Livestock: (as of 1973)
Pigs: 50,000
Cows: 1,300
Water buffaloes: 3,700

Insecticide: Commune used DDT and 666 powder, a form of DDT, which cost about US 10¢ to spray 1 *mou* of land

Average income at Kwang Li: RMB 1.30/day = US 65¢/day (US $19.50/month)
Average rice consumption: 53 *catties*/month

BIBLIOGRAPHY

Alley, Rewi. *Travels in China, 1966–71.* Peking: New World Press, 1973.

"A Visit to the Tungting People's Commune," *Peking Review.* Four parts:
"I—Its formation and growth." No. 13 (March 30, 1973), 14–15.
"II—A social structure combining government administration with commune management." No. 14 (April 6, 1973), 11–12, 23.
"III—Its three-level ownership." No. 15 (April 13, 1973), 11–12.
"IV—How a production team carries on its work." No. 16 (April 20, 1973), 26–28.

Barnett, A. Doak, ed. *Chinese Communist Politics in Action.* Seattle and London: University of Washington Press, 1969.

Ch'en, Jerome. *Mao and the Chinese Revolution.* London: Oxford University Press, 1965.

The Committee of Concerned Asian Scholars. *China! Inside the People's Republic.* New York, Toronto, and London: Bantam Books, 1972.

Crozier, Ralph S., ed. *China's Cultural Legacy and Communism.* New York: Praeger Publishers, 1970.

Fairbank, John King. *The United States and China,* third edition. Cambridge: Harvard University Press, 1971.

Fitzgerald, C. P. *The Birth of Communist China.* Harmondsworth, Middlesex: Penguin Books, 1964.

Hinton, William. *Fanshen: A Documentary of Revolution in a Chinese Village.* New York: Vintage Books, 1966.

Houn, Franklin W. *A Short History of Chinese Communism.* Englewood Cliffs, New Jersey: Prentice-Hall, 1967.

Mao Tse-tung. *Selected Readings from the Works of Mao Tse-tung.* Peking: Foreign Languages Press, 1971.

Myrdal, Jan. *Report from a Chinese Village.* New York: Signet Books, 1966.

————, and Gun Kessle. *China: The Revolution Continued.* London: Chatto & Windus, 1971.

Robottom, John. *China in Revolution from Sun Yat-sen to Mao Tse-tung.* New York: McGraw-Hill Book Company, 1967.

Schram, Stuart. *Mao Tse-tung.* Harmondsworth, Middlesex: Penguin Books, 1966.

Schurmann, Franz. *Ideology and Organization in Communist China,* second edition, enlarged. Berkeley and Los Angeles: University of California Press, 1968.

———, and Orville Schell, eds. *Communist China: Revolutionary Reconstruction and International Confrontation, 1949 to the Present.* New York: Vintage Books, 1967.

Snow, Edgar. *Red Star over China,* fifth printing. New York: Grove Press, Inc., 1961.

———. *The Long Revolution.* London: Hutchinson & Co. Ltd., 1973.

Yang, C. K. *Chinese Communist Society: The Family and the Village,* fifth paperback printing. Cambridge and London: The M.I.T. Press, 1972.